KENNETH C. DAVIS

ILLUSTRATED BY ROB SHEPPERSON

DON'T
KNOW
MUCH
ABOUT

Thomas Jefferson

HarperCollinsPublishers

Photo and Map Credits:

Page 32, Monticello/Thomas Jefferson Foundation, Inc.

All other photographs courtesy of the Library of Congress.

Maps on pages 14 and 106 by Patricia Tobin.

This is a Don't Know Much About® book.

Don't Know Much About® is the trademark of Kenneth C. Davis.

Don't Know Much About® Thomas Jefferson

Copyright © 2005 by Kenneth C. Davis

Library of Congress Cataloging-in-Publication Data

Davis, Kenneth C.

　Don't know much about Thomas Jefferson / Kenneth C. Davis ; illustrated by Rob
Shepperson.

　　p.　　cm. — (Don't know much about)

　Includes bibliographical references (p.　) and index.

　ISBN 0-06-028821-3 (lib. bdg.) — ISBN 0-06-442128-7 (pbk.)

　1. Jefferson, Thomas, 1743–1826—Juvenile literature.　2. Presidents—United States—
Biography—Juvenile literature.　I. Shepperson, Rob ill.　II. Title.

E332.79.D387 2005　　　　　　　　　　　　　　　　　　　　　　　　2004012492

973.4'6'092—dc22

Design by Charles Yuen
1 2 3 4 5 6 7 8 9 10
❖
First Edition

ACKNOWLEDGMENTS

An author's name goes on the cover of a book. But behind that book are a great many people who make it all happen. I would like to thank all the wonderful people at HarperCollins who helped make this book a reality, including Susan Katz, Kate Morgan Jackson, Barbara Lalicki, Martha Rago, Rosemary Brosnan, Amy Burton, Meredith Charpentier, Dana Hayward, Maggie Herold, Jeanne Hogle, Rachel Orr, Lorelei Russ, and Drew Willis. I would also like to thank David Black, Joy Tutela, and Alix Reid for their friendship, assistance, and great ideas. My wife, Joann, and my children, Jenny and Colin, are always a source of inspiration, joy, and support, and without them my work would not be possible.

I especially thank Gaye Wilson, Research Associate in the Monticello Research Department, for reviewing the manuscript and providing helpful insights; Sarah Thomson for researching the photos; Rob Shepperson for his striking illustrations; and April Prince for her unique contribution. This book would not have been possible without her tireless work, imagination, and creativity.

CONTENTS

Thomas Jefferson

"What do you want to be when you grow up?" Have you ever noticed that adults like to ask that question? Usually they expect kids to say things like doctor, firefighter, or teacher. But wouldn't they be surprised if you answered, "I am going to be a writer, a lawyer, a scientist, an architect, an inventor, a farmer, a diplomat, and start my own university. And, yeah, maybe I will be president too!"

Young Thomas Jefferson probably would not have given that answer as a kid in colonial America more than two hundred years ago. When he was a boy, there wasn't even a president! But Jefferson did all of this, and much more. After all, America's third president—the man whose face is on the front of a nickel—was an unusually talented person.

If the only thing Thomas Jefferson had ever done was write the Declaration of Independence, with those famous words "All Men are created equal," he would be known the world over as an inspiration to people who love freedom and democracy. But Jefferson was more than just a famous writer.

If he had only been president, we would remember him as a leader who expanded the nation with a famous land deal called the Louisiana Purchase. But he was more than just a clever politician.

If he had only designed and built his home called Monticello, he would be known as a great architect. And if Jefferson had only thought up such clever devices as a swivel chair, a dumbwaiter, and a revolving bookstand, he would be thought of as a remarkable inventor.

Writer, lawyer, scientist, architect, inventor, farmer, diplomat, philosopher, president—all of these words describe Jefferson. It makes you wonder if he ever had a moment's rest!

DON'T KNOW MUCH ABOUT® THOMAS JEFFERSON tells the story of one of the most fascinating and important people in America's past—a man whose life and words changed the world.

Like all the Don't Know Much About® books, this book asks questions, such as if Jefferson was a great president. But it also asks how the man who helped lead America's fight for freedom and liberty could keep slaves on his Virginia plantation. Because the story of Jefferson's life is also the story of a very different time in American history, this question doesn't have an easy answer. But asking questions—and thinking about the answers—is a fascinating way to get the true story of Thomas Jefferson, the man whose pen helped start a revolution.

CHAPTER 1

A Red-haired, Freckled Youth

Was Thomas Jefferson born in the United States?

On April 13, 1743, Thomas Jefferson was born in present-day Albemarle County, Virginia. But it wasn't part of the United States. Virginia was the first, largest, and richest of Britain's North American colonies. Its wealth was based on the tobacco plant. Early in the eighteenth century, Virginians were already looking west toward the Piedmont for land that hadn't been worn out by tobacco. The Jeffersons lived there in a roomy farmhouse named Shadwell, built by Thomas's father and several slaves, in the foothills of Virginia's Blue Ridge Mountains. Only about six years before, the Jeffersons had been some of the area's first settlers. There were barely any roads, nor any neighbors save Indians and wild animals.

COLONIES OF AN EMPIRE

When Thomas Jefferson was born, there wasn't yet a United States. Established in 1607, Virginia was one of thirteen separate British *colonies*, or lands controlled by another country, in North America. Although Great Britain, the island composed of England, Scotland, and Wales, was small (about the size of present-day Minnesota), it was a powerful empire. The British Empire was ruled by a king and *Parliament*, the group of leaders chosen to help a king make laws. So Thomas and his family were British citizens— subjects of the British king.

Was Thomas's family well-off?

The wealthiest Virginia families, some of whom owned hundreds of thousands of acres of land and hundreds of slaves, lived on huge *plantations* in the Tidewater region, near the Atlantic Ocean. Thomas's mother, Jane Randolph Jefferson, came from one of Virginia's most distinguished Tidewater families. About one hundred slaves staffed the grand Randolph home, which sat on a large plantation on the James River. The Randolphs' wealth, like that of other aristocrats, made them influential members of their community.

Thomas's father, Peter Jefferson, was not a Tidewater aristocrat but a smaller farmer and self-taught surveyor. A surveyor's job was to measure and map plots of land so they could be bought and sold. In a time when most of the land west

WHAT DOES IT MEAN?

In the southern colonies, where the land was fertile and the climate gentle, agriculture flourished. Crops like sugar, cotton, and tobacco were grown on large farms called **plantations**. Plantations were worked by slaves.

of the Blue Ridge was unmapped, this was an important job. When Thomas was six, Peter ventured deep into the wilderness to help make the first accurate map of Virginia.

So Thomas was born into the upper class, by virtue of his mother—but he always had the independent, self-reliant streak of his father. The Jeffersons were not as well-off as some Virginians, but they were always comfortable. Thomas was raised in the style of a country gentleman.

I.O.U. . . . FIVE HUNDRED POUNDS OF TOBACCO?

A colonial Virginian who wanted to buy a horse, acquire new books, or pay his taxes might do so with English pounds, shillings, and pence, or with coins from Spain, France, or Portugal. But hard cash was scarce. What *wasn't* scarce was tobacco, Virginia's most valuable cash crop. So tobacco was used as money. Rather than carry around tobacco leaves, a person made purchases with a tobacco certificate. In much the same way we write checks to transfer money from our bank accounts into others', a tobacco certificate transferred a certain amount of tobacco in the warehouse from one person to another. Whoever held the certificate owned the tobacco.

What was Thomas's earliest memory?

When Thomas was two, his father's closest friend, William Randolph, died. The Jeffersons moved to Randolph's plantation, called Tuckahoe, to care for his lands and children. They would stay for seven years.

Thomas's earliest memory was being lifted up to a slave on horseback and sitting on a pillow for the

ride to Tuckahoe. The mud
trails that passed for roads
were so rough that the
fifty-mile trip took three
days.

At Tuckahoe there
were more playmates
than there had been
at Shadwell. In
addition to Thomas's
three sisters, there were
two Randolph girls and
one boy (also named
Thomas), and many slave
children.

Where was Thomas's first school?

When Thomas was five, he joined his two older
sisters, the three Randolph children, and their tutor
in a small building near the main house at
Tuckahoe. Thomas loved to read and write, and his
parents could tell that he was bright. When the
Jeffersons moved back to Shadwell, nine-year-old
Thomas stayed near Tuckahoe and boarded at a
Latin school. There he learned French and the
classics (ancient Greek and Roman texts). These
were subjects young men of the upper class were
expected to know. While learning all those new
words was overwhelming at first, Thomas would be
glad for it later: "To read the Latin and Greek
authors in their original is a sublime luxury," he
wrote.

What did young Thomas think of slavery?

Slavery had been part of Virginia life almost since
the first blacks were brought from Africa in 1619.
(These blacks were listed as servants, but they were
soon treated as slaves.) Black slaves served and
cared for Thomas from the moment he was born to
the day he died, and slave children were among his
earliest friends.

Though it may have been difficult for Thomas to
understand why his black friends couldn't go to
school with him, it seems that Thomas was isolated
from the worst parts of slavery. Peter Jefferson did
not see blacks as his equals, but neither did he beat
his slaves or treat them like animals, the way some
slave owners did. Of course, Peter did profit from his
slaves' labor, especially from the tobacco they grew
at Shadwell.

Did Thomas have any brothers?

Thomas eventually had six sisters and three
brothers, but two of his brothers died at Tuckahoe.

This was not unusual in Thomas's day. Only one in three children survived childhood diseases such as whooping cough, measles, mumps, and scarlet fever. Doctors back then did not understand germs, so there wasn't a great deal they could do to help their patients. Some treatments, like bloodletting—bleeding a vein with the hope that it would let an illness drain out—could actually make the patient worse.

Of Thomas's seven surviving siblings, his older sister Jane was his favorite. When Thomas came home to Shadwell for summer and holiday breaks, he and Jane took long walks through the forest together. The two of them shared a love of books and music, and Jane encouraged her brother in both.

Did Thomas ever fiddle around?

Music was an important part of social life in colonial days. Most well-educated colonists could read music and play an instrument such as the flute, guitar, harpsichord, harp, guitar, or violin. Thomas learned to play the violin, commonly called the fiddle. He often accompanied Jane while she sang.

Thomas became an accomplished amateur violinist who sometimes spent three hours a day practicing. Through much of his life, he would use music to take his mind off the "cares of the day." In addition to playing his fiddle, Thomas was said to have a pleasant voice and frequently sang to himself while he rode or walked about.

Jefferson's America

New York City

PENNSYLVANIA

Delaware River

Philadelphia

NEW JERSEY

DELAWARE

Potomac River

Annapolis

MARYLAND

Mount Vernon
Shadwell
Charlottesville
Monticello
Elk Hill
Richmond
Williamsburg
Yorktown
Poplar Forest
James River
Tuckahoe

VIRGINIA

BLUE RIDGE MOUNTAINS

NORTH
CAROLINA

Atlantic Ocean

N

Did Thomas Jefferson know any Indians?

While Peter Jefferson was exploring and surveying his lands, he had made many Indian friends. It wasn't unusual for one hundred Cherokees to visit Shadwell and camp near the house. In a day when most white settlers thought Indians were dangerous savages, Peter Jefferson treated them with respect. Thomas did the same. He admired the Indians' dignity, strength, and intelligence.

SURPRISE SLEEPOVERS IN OLD VIRGINIA!

In the southern colonies, it was customary for travelers to stop at private homes for meals or overnight lodging. (In towns travelers often stayed at inns or taverns instead.) A family never knew who might drop in, or for how long; friends and strangers alike might stay for dinner, or for a few days or even weeks. Colonial Virginians welcomed visitors and the news and varied conversation they brought. During Thomas's youth, many travelers to and from Williamsburg, Virginia's colonial capital, stopped at Shadwell because it was near a main road.

Did Thomas get along with his parents?

We know very little about Thomas's relationship with his mother, but it's clear that Thomas revered his father and learned much from him. Though Peter Jefferson lacked formal education, Thomas remembered that "he read much and improved himself."

On summer days in the woods near Shadwell, Thomas learned to ride, shoot, hunt, swim, and row a canoe. Soon red-haired, freckled Thomas was nearly as tall and strong as his father. It appears that Peter Jefferson encouraged Thomas to record

what he observed in nature—the color and texture of animals and the appearance of seasonal plants and flowers.

Not all lessons took place out-of-doors. Peter Jefferson showed Thomas that with privilege came duty. In Virginia the men of the planter class were expected to participate in the colony's government. At various times Peter Jefferson served as county sheriff, justice of the peace, and lieutenant colonel of the militia. In 1754 he was elected by his neighbors to represent Albemarle County in the Virginia House of Burgesses, the body of representatives that helped the colonial governor make laws.

What did Thomas Jefferson become when he was fourteen?

In the summer of 1757, Peter Jefferson suddenly fell ill and died, leaving fourteen-year-old Thomas the man of the family. Never having turned to his mother for guidance, Thomas felt utterly alone.

Among the things Peter Jefferson left Thomas in his will were his books, his mathematical instruments, a slave named Sawney, and a choice between two handsome parcels of land. Thomas chose 2,650 acres on which sat both Shadwell and a favorite hill Thomas called his "little mountain." This land, along with farm animals and at least twenty additional slaves, would become his when he turned twenty-one.

Peter Jefferson's will named several men to oversee his estate and act as guardians of his children. The will also requested that Thomas receive a "thorough classical education." Thomas's mother and guardians arranged for him to study with Reverend James Maury, who lived fourteen miles from Shadwell. During the week Thomas and his fellow students studied the classics, history, philosophy, and natural science. On weekends Thomas rode home to help his mother and keep an eye on his siblings.

What was Thomas Jefferson's first big adventure?

After two years of studying with Reverend Maury, Thomas told his guardians he wanted to attend the College of William and Mary in Williamsburg. Established in 1693, "the College," as William and Mary was known among Virginians, was the second-oldest college in America after Harvard University.

In March 1760 Thomas and his personal servant, a slave named Jupiter, set out for the capital. Thomas had never been to a city, and the sights and sounds enchanted him. Though Williamsburg was smaller than Boston, New York, or Philadelphia, the capital of Virginia was an important center of trade, culture, and government. Home to about one thousand people, Williamsburg (named for King William III of England) boasted fine shops, renowned theaters, several taverns, and the grand governor's palace. The town's main thoroughfare, stately Duke of Gloucester Street, stretched a mile from the capitol building in the east to the three college buildings in the west. In between were public buildings, the market square, tradesmen's shops, and the office of the *Virginia Gazette*. Thomas always loved books, and his favorite shop was the bookstore.

Horses, wagons, farmers' carts, and elegant carriages kicked up dust as they traveled along the city streets. On foot were bustling college students, frontiersmen, slaves, Indians, and government leaders. Strolling more leisurely were full-skirted women and men in knee breeches and long, formfitting waistcoats—the latest fashions from London (though in fabrics better suited to the warm Virginia climate).

What did Thomas do during his first term in college?

Thomas made friends easily in Williamsburg. Though many people said he was reserved and aloof at first meeting, they generally agreed he was amiable, easygoing, and remarkably intelligent once they'd spent more time with him. Thomas was unusually tall for his day (just over six feet two inches) and a bit lanky, with large hands and feet. He was ruggedly handsome, with bright gray eyes, fair skin but ever-rosy cheeks, and thick reddish blond hair he wore pulled back loosely behind his neck. Wealthy men of the day often wore wigs or powdered their hair, but Thomas seldom did.

With his new friends, Thomas took advantage of Williamsburg's many attractions. He went to horse races and concerts. He saw his first play. He attended dances at the Raleigh Tavern, stepping in time to the popular minuets and reels of the day. In all, Thomas did a lot of playing—but not much studying—his first term.

Where did Thomas get his real college education?

After his first term, Thomas resolved to buckle down. He still had fun, but he also studied hard.

Thomas's favorite professor was his mathematics instructor, Dr. William Small. Dr. Small's zest for learning aroused Thomas's own passion for new ideas, and the two men spent many hours outside the classroom discussing logic, philosophy, and scholarship. Thomas said Dr. Small set him on a course of learning and observation that he followed the rest of his life.

Dr. Small opened additional doors for Thomas by introducing him to other learned and distinguished men: Virginia's governor, Francis Fauquier, and the colony's most esteemed lawyer, George Wythe. Impressed by the eighteen-year-old student's uncommon curiosity and intellect, Governor

Fauquier invited Thomas to dine weekly at the governor's palace and to play in an amateur chamber ensemble. This extraordinary privilege exposed young Thomas to a broad range of ideas about science, art, politics—ideas that made him realize that the world was larger than his Virginia. More than the classroom, Thomas later said, it was "to the habitual conversations of these occasions I owed much instruction." Thomas Jefferson was growing up.

AMERICAN VOICES

66 When I . . . recollect the various sorts of bad company with which I associated from time to time, I am astonished I did not turn off with some of them, and become as worthless to society as they were. I had the good fortune to become acquainted very early with some characters of very high standing, and to feel the incessant wish that I could ever become what they were. 99

—**Jefferson**, writing to his grandson Thomas Jefferson Randolph about his own youth, in 1808

Was the Enlightenment a new kind of light fixture?

The ideas to which Dr. Small introduced Jefferson included those of the Enlightenment, a philosophical and intellectual movement of the seventeenth and eighteenth centuries. Before this time, most people simply believed what the Church had taught for more than a thousand years: that divine forces ruled the world. During the

Enlightenment some people reasoned that the universe was ruled by natural laws that made sense and could be understood by observation and scientific inquiry. Scientists like Isaac Newton explained the universe in terms of math and physics, not superstition or religion. The universe was no longer just what a church said it was.

Enlightenment thinkers believed in the power and freedom of the human mind. They argued that people were basically good and, if educated about the laws of nature, could use those laws to run their own governments and societies. One Enlightenment thinker in England, John Locke, said that a government's power came from what the people— not a church or a king—told it to do.

While Enlightenment thinkers in Europe were writing scholarly works on individual rights, Virginians were experiencing these things firsthand simply by managing their own farms and plantations and electing burgesses to write laws on their behalf. The Enlightenment, which is also called the Age of Reason, struck a chord with Jefferson; to him these ideals simply made sense.

VOICES FROM HISTORY

❝ Since all governments exist for men, not men for governments, all governments derive their just powers from the consent of the governed. ❞
—English philosopher **John Locke** (1632–1704)

What did Thomas Jefferson often do more than fifteen hours a day in Williamsburg?

After two years at William and Mary, Jefferson began to study law under George Wythe. In Jefferson's day students learned the law by reading, watching, and assisting an established lawyer. (Students of trades such as printing, blacksmithing, and carpentry also learned by apprenticeship.) Jefferson did research for Wythe, attended sessions of the General Court and House of Burgesses, and read and reread the law books Wythe recommended. As Jefferson had done while studying with Dr. Small, he recorded in a "commonplace book" the main ideas of what he was reading. This helped him clarify his thoughts.

Jefferson spent five years, rather than the usual two, preparing himself to practice law. He believed that a good lawyer, like any learned man of his day, should possess thorough knowledge of science, history, geography, and languages. Sometimes Jefferson studied from dawn until 2 A.M. He followed a strict schedule of reading, stopping only in the late afternoons to run a mile into the country and back for exercise. Loyal Jupiter made sure Jefferson ate his meals.

CHAPTER 2

Becoming an American

Protesting the
Stamp Act

What British laws didn't get the colonists' stamp of approval?

While Jefferson was studying law, the relationship between Britain and its American colonies began to sour. From 1756 to 1763, longtime-foes Britain and France fought in a conflict that was known in Europe as the Seven Years' War. The war was also fought in North America, where it was called the French and Indian War. Britain and France and their respective Indian *allies*, or friends, vied for control of the continent.

Britain eventually won the war and sent the French packing from Canada. But the fighting had been costly. To raise money, Britain's king, George III, and Parliament decided to tax the colonists. After all, the debts had been incurred partly in the colonists' defense. And British troops were still protecting America's western frontier; somehow these troops had to be paid.

The British taxes came in the form of the Sugar Act (1764) and the Stamp Act (1765). The Sugar Act taxed sugar, coffee, and wine imported to the colonies from Britain. The Stamp Act taxed everything printed on paper, from newspapers to marriage licenses to playing cards. The Stamp Act was the first time Parliament had taxed the colonists directly on goods produced and sold within the colonies. This was a serious break with tradition. Before the Stamp Act, internal taxes had been collected only by the colonial legislatures.

Nearly all colonists were loyal British citizens who didn't mind paying their share for the war. But they *did* object to not being asked about it. The colonists had no representation in Parliament as their British counterparts across the ocean did. They wanted to have a say in how they were governed.

What did colonists say about the British taxes?

The Stamp Act outraged most colonists. The rallying cry "no taxation without representation" rang out at many a riot and demonstration.

In Virginia the House of Burgesses was silent about the Stamp Act until Jefferson's friend Patrick Henry, a newly elected burgess, raised the issue. Jefferson had first met Henry, a man seven years his senior, at the plantation of a mutual friend in 1759. Though Henry was unconcerned with book learning or a tidy appearance, Jefferson was drawn to his outgoing nature and powerful way of speaking.

Now Henry stood before the House and presented ideas that others had been too afraid to discuss, even among themselves: The colonists, as British citizens, were entitled to the same freedoms as if they had been born in England. One of these freedoms, Henry said, was that people should be governed by their own assemblies. Therefore, only the Virginia legislature had the right to impose internal taxes on Virginians.

These were radical words. Some burgesses interrupted with cries of "Treason! Treason!"

"If this be treason, make the most of it!" Henry supposedly replied.

Listening at the door was twenty-two-year-old Thomas Jefferson.

> **WHAT DOES IT MEAN?**
> **Treason** is betrayal of your country, especially by waging war against it. In Britain treason was punishable by death.

❝ At the door of the lobby of the House of Burgesses, [I] heard the splendid display of Mr. Henry's talents as a popular orator. They were great indeed; such as I have never heard from any other man. ❞

—**Jefferson**, on hearing Patrick Henry speak against the Stamp Act, in 1765

Did the colonists "lick" the Stamp Act?

After Patrick Henry delivered his fiery words, Virginians began to take sides in the budding conflict: Whigs, or Patriots, wanted to stand up for their rights; Tories, or Loyalists, supported the British Crown. As tensions mounted in the coming years, Jefferson would land squarely with the Patriots.

Word of Henry's defiant speech spread by newspapers and word of mouth during the summer of 1765, helping unite Patriots in other colonies. Many Patriots encouraged colonists to boycott, or refuse to buy, British imports. Parliament wouldn't listen to the colonists, but it did listen to the British merchants who protested the income they lost to the boycott. The Stamp Act was repealed, or taken back, in 1766. But the conflict had just begun.

Why did "homespun" become fashionable in Virginia?

In the wake of the protests against the Stamp Act, Parliament passed another kind of tax, one they hoped the colonists wouldn't notice. The Townshend Acts (1767) taxed tea, lead, paint, paper, and glass imported into the colonies. This time, however, the tax was paid by merchants who imported the goods, not the individuals who bought them.

The colonists saw through this scheme and again cried "no taxation without representation." When the Massachusetts legislature sent a petition to the other colonial legislatures, seeking a united front against the Townshend Acts, Parliament ruled such petitions treasonous. The House of Burgesses passed resolutions restating its sole right to tax Virginians and asserting its freedom to join the other colonies in asking for their rights. In response, Virginia's colonial governor dissolved the House of Burgesses.

The defiant burgesses continued to meet as an unofficial body at Williamsburg's Raleigh Tavern. There they drew up an agreement to boycott a long list of British imports: paper, wine, oil, sugar, cloth, leather, fruit, meat, and other goods. The idea was to stop all trade with Britain until Parliament repealed the hated taxes. In Williamsburg it became fashionable to wear clothing made of plain "homespun" rather than elegant English silks. Throughout the colonies people drank "liberty tea" made of home-grown raspberry, strawberry, or mint leaves, rather than buy the imported tea taxed by the British.

How did Jefferson put all his studying to use?

In 1767 Jefferson passed the required exams to become a lawyer. He established a successful law practice, trying cases in the General Court and in the smaller county courts.

The following year Jefferson was elected to the House of Burgesses for the term beginning in 1769. Jefferson was generally quiet in sessions and committees, learning from the older and more experienced burgesses around him. When Jefferson drafted a bill to make it easier for slave owners to free slaves (at the time Virginia slaves could only be freed for having performed "meritorious service"), he learned that some of his ideas differed significantly from those of the more established Tidewater burgesses. They soundly defeated the bill, preferring to keep things as they were.

What else was on Jefferson's mind these days?

Jefferson had come into his inheritance in 1764, when he turned twenty-one. In 1768 he broke ground for a new house atop his "little mountain" near Shadwell. As a boy Jefferson had dreamed of building a home on this majestic spot he now called Monticello ("little mountain" in Italian).

Building a home on top of a hill was uncommon at the time. Without modern roads or transportation, getting everything—water, building materials, furniture, and eventually friends and family—up the steep mountainside was a chore. Roads had to be carved to the summit and the mountaintop cleared and leveled. But for Jefferson the extra costs and extra effort, for himself and for his slaves and hired hands, would be worth it.

Who designed Jefferson's house?

He did—every detail. There were no professional architects in the colonies at the time, so Jefferson taught himself everything he needed to know. He sought out every book on the subject and read it more than once. Jefferson became a designer, draftsman, and engineer. In designing his home, he was seeking simplicity, grace, dignity, and durability. He combined the designs of the buildings and houses he had seen with those he knew from books, especially the works of the sixteenth-century Italian architect Andrea Palladio. Jefferson called the result, Monticello, his "essay in architecture"—an expression of who he was. When something didn't suit his taste or meet his expectation, he had it torn down and started over.

COLONIAL PLANTERS: JACKS-OF-ALL-TRADES

In colonial America, planters managed large tracts of land and groups of workers, and were responsible for the productivity and well-being of both. Since plantations were largely self-sufficient, many planters had little choice but to learn about business, agriculture, medicine, botany, law, architecture, and carpentry. What was unusual about Jefferson's broad range of knowledge was the depth to which he explored, pondered, and understood the many topics he studied. Jefferson knew a great deal about many different subjects and could put his great knowledge to practical use at Monticello.

Did Jefferson plan to live at Monticello alone?

The twenty or so slaves Jefferson had inherited from his father would live at Monticello. And more and more, Jefferson was looking for a wife.

Jefferson's only real romance had been when he fell for a young woman named Rebecca Burwell during his college days. For a year he'd done little to act upon his feelings; when he did, he became so tongue-tied he could barely speak. Jefferson was now more mature and confident around women. He was a burgess, a respectable lawyer, and a landowner. He was ready to be married. And he was in love.

Where did Jefferson meet his future bride?

In Williamsburg in 1770, twenty-seven-year-old Jefferson met Martha Wayles Skelton, the wealthy daughter of a Virginia lawyer and a widow seven years his junior. Jefferson fell hard and fast for the petite beauty. More than her handsome appearance, though, it was Martha's intelligence, lively spirit, and love of music to which Jefferson was attracted.

THE SONGBIRD-LOVEBIRDS

Jefferson had competition in winning Martha's heart, for there were many men eager to marry her. According to family lore, Thomas was visiting Martha at her home when two other young men happened to arrive simultaneously. Standing outside, they heard Thomas and Martha playing music and singing a love song. After listening a bit, the suitors left, deciding to pursue Martha no longer. Was it the song the young couple was singing, the emotion in their voices, or something else entirely? We can only imagine.

Jefferson called often at Martha's father's house, called the Forest. There the couple would sing, or Martha would accompany Thomas on the harpsichord while he played his violin. Jefferson also enjoyed discussing books and ideas with Martha, who read and wrote better than many women of her day. On New Year's Day, 1772, the two were married before a houseful of guests at the Forest.

What was the Jeffersons' "honeymoon lodge"?

More than two weeks of dancing, feasting, and celebration followed Thomas and Martha's wedding. Finally, the newlyweds set out for Monticello in a small horse-drawn carriage. Snow flurries fell around them, adding to the feeling of romance.

By the time the couple approached Monticello, the flurries had become a blizzard. Thomas and Martha abandoned their carriage and continued on horseback, struggling up the mountain in three feet of snow—"the deepest snow we have ever seen," Thomas later wrote. Though the foundation of Jefferson's mountaintop home had been laid in 1770, the only completed structure was the southwest pavilion, a tiny, one-room cottage where he had been living. It was hardly a suitable home for his new bride, but Shadwell had burned two years earlier. The cottage was his only option. Arriving at night, Thomas built a fire in the cottage and the newlyweds made a cozy "honeymoon lodge." Ahead lay what Jefferson would call "years of unchequered happiness."

Did Thomas and Martha have any children?

Patsy Jefferson

Thomas and Martha's first child, a girl named Martha (later called Patsy), was born in September 1772. Four more daughters and one son would follow over the next ten years. However, only two of these six children—Patsy and Mary (who went by Polly, then Maria)—would live past the age of three.

Why did Boston Patriots throw a tea party in 1773?

Jefferson had taken some time off from politics to enjoy married life, but the politics continued on. Pressured by British merchants whose goods the colonists were boycotting, Parliament had repealed the Townshend Acts, except for the tax on tea, in 1770. Parliament kept the one tax to prove that Britain could still tax the colonists. Many colonists drank tea daily, so the tax was especially irritating. And as Jefferson saw it, one tax was as bad as many; the issues of taxation and British interference in colonial affairs were the same.

When an additional tea tax was imposed by the Tea Act in 1773, about 150 Bostonians disguised as Indians boarded tea-laden British ships in Boston Harbor to dump the contents of 342 chests of tea into the sea. When King George heard about the "Tea Party," he was furious. Parliament responded by cracking down on hotheaded Boston. It banned town meetings so colonists couldn't make their own laws. It required Bostonians to feed and house thousands of British troops sent to keep order. Perhaps worst of all, Parliament closed Boston Harbor until the tea was paid for, threatening Bostonians with starvation: No food could enter the city by ship. Colonists called these orders the "Intolerable Acts."

❝ The die is now cast. The colonies must either submit or triumph. ❞

—**King George III**, after Parliament passed the "Intolerable Acts," in 1774

How did the Boston Tea Party affect colonists in Virginia?

After Parliament closed Boston Harbor, the other colonies jumped to aid Massachusetts by sending food, clothing, and prayers. Each colony realized it could be the next target of Parliament's harsh treatment. More and more, colonists were beginning to think of themselves as "Americans" rather than "Virginians" or "New Yorkers."

Just months before the Tea Party, Jefferson and four other young burgesses had proposed the creation of intercolonial "committees of correspondence." These committees would keep colonial leaders abreast of what was happening elsewhere. An express rider from the Boston committee had brought the news of the harbor's closing to Williamsburg. In response to the Tea Party, Jefferson proposed a day of fasting and prayer in Virginia. He and other burgesses also suggested that delegates from every colony meet in Philadelphia, Pennsylvania, that fall. At this First Continental Congress, delegates would address the colonies' common concerns.

CHAPTER 3

The Pen of the Revolution

Declaration of Independence by John Trumbull

Did Jefferson attend the First Continental Congress?

The members of the House of Burgesses, still meeting as an official body, didn't elect Jefferson a delegate to the Continental Congress; he was still a young and relatively new member of their ranks. But thanks to some of Jefferson's colleagues, the words and ideas he had written to guide the Virginia delegation's contributions to an address to King George did make their way to Philadelphia. Jefferson outlined Britain's abuses of the colonies and argued that Parliament had no authority over them because the relationship between the colonies and their mother country was a voluntary one. Jefferson

35

appealed to King George to give the colonists the rights they deserved as British citizens and to be a servant, not an oppressor, of his people. These ideas were revolutionary in a day when most countries were governed by monarchs (kings, queens, emperors, or other unelected rulers), who were used to being treated with reverence.

Jefferson sent the resolutions from Monticello to Williamsburg rather than deliver them himself, because he had fallen ill. When his fellow burgesses read the resolutions, many thought they were too radical. But those who did approve titled the resolutions *Summary View of the Rights of British America* and had them printed. The document would make Jefferson known throughout the colonies—and in England, where his name was put on a list of dangerous American rebels.

AMERICAN VOICES

66 The principles of common sense . . . must be surrendered up, before his Majesty's subjects here, can be persuaded to believe, that they hold their political existence at the will of a British Parliament . . . a body of men whom they never saw, in whom they never confided, and over whom they have no powers of punishment or removal. . . . The God who gave us life, gave us liberty at the same time. 99
          —**Jefferson**, *Summary View of the Rights of British America*, 1774

What did the First Continental Congress do?

Fifty-five delegates from every colony but Georgia met in Philadelphia in September 1774. Among them were Virginians George Washington and Patrick

Henry; Massachusetts cousins John and Samuel Adams; and the famous writer-scientist-inventor Benjamin Franklin of Pennsylvania.

Congress drew up a Declaration of Rights and Grievances to be sent to their unruly ruler, King George. With this document they hoped to restore the colonists' rights as British citizens and to restore harmony with the British Crown. Congress also organized a boycott of imports from and exports to Britain and stated that if British soldiers stationed in Boston attacked the Patriots, all the colonies would consider themselves attacked. The colonial front was united.

Was Jefferson always gung ho for independence?

Jefferson remained a loyal British citizen as he penned *Summary View*. Yet he was also a staunch supporter of colonial rights, largely because he believed that the natural rights and self-government the Patriots sought were justly theirs under British common law. Jefferson would say that whenever a government neglects to protect the rights of its citizens, the citizens have the right to change or abolish it and create a new government. Jefferson never liked war or violence. But the more King George dug in his heels, the more Jefferson became convinced that war was coming, like it or not.

Most delegates in Congress were more cautious, believing that friendship could be restored if Britain would stop meddling in American affairs. But there were some radicals who, like Jefferson, could see that this was highly unlikely. These delegates began to feel that separation or independence was inevitable, but they held their tongues. If they spoke of such things too early and caused an uproar, their cause might be lost altogether.

66 There is not in the British empire, a man who more cordially loves a union with Great Britain than I do. But by the God that made me, I will cease to exist before I yield to a connection on such terms as the British Parliament propose. 99

—**Jefferson**, in a letter to his cousin John Randolph, who had recently moved to London because he didn't agree with the rebellious colonists, in 1775

Why was a Second Continental Congress necessary?

Congress had agreed to meet again in May 1775 if little progress had been made. Indeed, by that time, things had gotten worse. King George had ignored the Declaration of Rights and Grievances, saying only that anyone who didn't agree with him was a "traitor and a scoundrel." By the time the Second Continental Congress met, shots had been fired between British *redcoats* and Massachusetts *minutemen* at Lexington and Concord, northwest of Boston, and King George had declared the colonies in a state of rebellion. Now colonial troops were drilling outside the Pennsylvania State House in Philadelphia, where Congress met. Patriots were gathering war supplies.

> **WHAT DOES IT MEAN?**
>
> **Redcoats** were British soldiers, so named for the color of their uniforms. Some Patriots called them "lobsterbacks."
>
> **Minutemen** generally had no uniforms at all. These Massachusetts Patriots were farmers and tradesmen with little military training who were said to be ready to pick up their guns on a minute's notice.

In June Congress voted to establish a Continental army. George Washington was chosen unanimously to lead it. Two days later, before General Washington could depart for Massachusetts, the first organized fighting of the rebellion took place on Breed's Hill outside Boston

(commonly known as the Battle of Bunker Hill). Within months, thousands of the king's soldiers would arrive in their colonies.

Yet many colonists, and still a good number of congressmen, hoped to resolve things without further bloodshed. The most outspoken of those opposed to severing ties, Congressman John Dickinson of Pennsylvania, wrote one last proposal to King George on behalf of the Congress. This Olive Branch Petition would get Congress no further than its first appeal had.

Why did Jefferson arrive late at the Second Continental Congress?

In March 1775 Jefferson was selected as an alternate to the Second Continental Congress. When Virginia's colonial governor called an emergency session of the House of Burgesses, delegate Peyton Randolph was summoned back to Virginia to preside over the session. Jefferson left to take Randolph's place in Philadelphia.

Congress had been in session several weeks when Jefferson, appearing the perfect Virginia gentleman, arrived on June 20. Accompanied by three slaves, he rode into the city in an elegant carriage pulled by four horses.

Philadelphia was North America's largest city and busiest port. Lumber, iron, and wheat were sent from docks on the Delware River to England. Ships filled with sugar, molasses, spices, and newcomers to America arrived every day. The city's wide streets, always bustling with people, were lined with fancy shops, taverns, coffeehouses, printers, booksellers, and churches. It was a far cry from Jefferson's quiet country life in Virginia.

In Congress, thanks in part to *Summary View*, Jefferson was known to be a radical and an excellent writer. At age thirty-two he was one of the youngest, and quietest, delegates. John Adams, with whom Jefferson would serve on many committees, later wrote, "During the whole time I sat with him in Congress, I never heard him utter three sentences together." But Adams praised his younger colleague for being "prompt, frank, explicit, and decisive upon committees and in conversation." Jefferson's talents would be put to use immediately.

Why did Jefferson's family need him in winter and spring of 1776?

In November 1775 word arrived in Philadelphia that King George had rejected the Olive Branch Petition. In so doing, the king was choosing to fight the colonists, although no formal declaration of war had been issued by either side.

Congress, its members tired and frustrated, called a short recess for the Christmas holiday. Jefferson took an extended leave because his wife and mother were ill. Martha Jefferson was both sick and deeply depressed, for the couple's seventeen-month-old daughter, Jane, had died in September. Jefferson did everything he could to cheer, console, and care for his beloved wife. He also kept an eye on his mother, whose health was failing; she died of a stroke a few months later. Because of all the strain, Jefferson developed a migraine headache, an ailment that often plagued him in stressful times, and was forced to remain at Monticello for another several weeks. When he departed for Congress at the beginning of May 1776, he wished Martha would accompany him. But she was still too frail. Though upset about leaving her, Jefferson felt it was his duty to go.

What did Patriot Thomas Paine think was common sense?

Though Jefferson was late returning to Congress, he had kept up with events in Philadelphia via letters and newspapers. He also read a little book called *Common Sense*, which had been published in January. In *Common Sense*, author Thomas Paine argued that it made sense for the American colonies to be free and independent from Britain. Monarchy was no good; Britain's taxes and trade restrictions were bad for the American economy; it was silly for a tiny island three thousand miles away to rule a vast continent. Some colonists had been thinking this way, but it was the first time such thoughts had been published. The pamphlet was an instant best-seller and an enormous boost to the Patriot cause. Congress inched toward declaring independence. Before Jefferson left Virginia, he took an informal poll of his neighbors and concluded that nine out of ten favored independence.

What document is a sort of American national birth certificate?

On June 7, soon after Jefferson returned to Philadelphia, the Virginia delegates presented a motion "to declare the United Colonies free and independent states." Congress faced a history-making decision, one that could pit the colonies against the mightiest power in the world.

Debate on the motion began the next day and continued past dark. With no consensus in sight, the vote over whether to accept the motion was postponed until July 1; with an issue so important, it was essential that the vote be unanimous. In the meantime, a committee was created to draw up a Declaration of Independence. That way, no time would be lost if the motion passed.

The Declaration was to announce the colonies' separation from Britain and tell the world, clearly and simply, what the colonists were fighting for. Congress also hoped the document would inspire the colonists and encourage support from other nations. The committee appointed to draft the Declaration included Congressmen John Adams, Benjamin Franklin, Roger Sherman of Connecticut, Robert Livingston of New York—and Thomas Jefferson.

Thomas Jefferson holds a draft of the Declaration.

Why was Jefferson chosen to write the Declaration of Independence?

How the committee decided Jefferson would draft the document wasn't recorded at the time, though it likely had something to do with what John Adams called Jefferson's "happy talent of composition." Both Adams and Jefferson recalled the event much later, with different explanations. Adams wrote that Jefferson proposed that Adams do it, but that he insisted upon Jefferson. Jefferson, on the other hand, remembered that the committee asked him to do it alone, and he accepted: "I consented: I drew it [up]."

❝You should do it," Jefferson said.

"Oh! No," Adams replied.

"Why will you not?" Jefferson asked. "You ought to do it."

"I will not."

"Why?"

"Reasons enough."

"What can be your reasons?"

"Reason 1st. You are a Virginian, and a Virginian ought to appear at the head of this business. Reason 2nd. I am obnoxious, suspected, and unpopular. You are very much otherwise. Reason 3rd. You can write ten times better than I can."

"Well, if you are decided, I will do as well as I can. ❞

—**John Adams**, describing his memory of the conversation that led to Jefferson drafting the Declaration of Independence, in 1822

How long did it take Jefferson to write the Declaration?

Jefferson composed the Declaration in his lodgings on the corner of Seventh and Market Streets, a few blocks from the State House. In his second-floor rooms, the windows opened for cross ventilation against the dreadful Philadelphia heat, Jefferson rose before dawn. He soaked his feet in a basin of cold water, a practice he believed prevented colds. After a breakfast of tea and biscuits, and perhaps a little quiet playing of his violin, he sat down to write. Working at a portable desk he had designed himself, Jefferson scratched steadily across the paper with his quill pen. He crossed out and revised as he went, recopying drafts when they were too messy to read. Jefferson consulted no books; all the information he needed had been in his head for years. It was hot, solitary work, but it suited him.

Jefferson completed his task in seventeen days. He showed his draft to Adams and Franklin, the two "whose opinions I most wanted." They made several small changes, which Sherman and Livingston approved.

What does the Declaration of Independence say?

The Declaration laid out the argument for why America should make the break with Great Britain. Jefferson accused King George and Parliament of more than two dozen offenses. The Declaration also said that, because the king refused to address the colonists' grievances, the colonists were asserting their right to abolish the union with the mother country and form a new, independent nation. Perhaps the Declaration's most radical idea was the now-famous assertion that "all Men are created equal, that they are endowed by their Creator with certain unalienable Rights, that among these are Life, Liberty, and the Pursuit of Happiness."

❝ When in the Course of human Events, it becomes necessary for one People to dissolve the Political Bands which have connected them with another . . . a decent Respect to the Opinions of Mankind requires that they should declare the causes which impel them to the Separation.

"We hold these Truths to be self-evident, that all Men are created equal, that they are endowed by their Creator with certain unalienable Rights, that among these are Life, Liberty, and the Pursuit of Happiness—That to secure these Rights, Governments are instituted among Men, deriving their Powers from the Consent of the Governed, that whenever any Form of Government becomes destructive of these Ends, it is the Right of the People to alter or abolish it, and to institute new Government. . . .

"We therefore, the Representatives of the UNITED STATES OF AMERICA, in GENERAL CONGRESS Assembled, appealing to the Supreme Judge of the World for the Rectitude of our Intentions, do, in the Name, and by the Authority of the good People of these Colonies, solemnly Publish and Declare, That these United Colonies are, and by Right ought to be, FREE AND INDEPENDENT STATES; that they are absolved from all Allegiance to the British Crown, and that all political Connection between them and the State of Great-Britain, is and ought to be totally dissolved. . . . ❞

—From the **Declaration of Independence**

Did Congress think the Declaration was word perfect?

On July 2, 1776, Congress voted to accept Virginia's proposed motion for independence. The break was

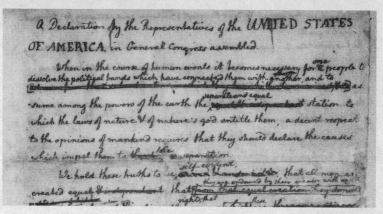

made! Then the delegates turned their attention to Jefferson's Declaration. The author sat in uneasy silence as Congress went over the document word by word, debating, criticizing, revising. The process took the better part of three days. Benjamin Franklin tried to comfort the agonized Jefferson by telling him a humorous story of a hatter's sign that was edited so many times it was reduced to the man's name and a picture of a hat. Though Jefferson appreciated Franklin's efforts to cheer him, it was John Adams who made him feel better. Adams fought passionately for every word of Jefferson's Declaration and was "the pillar of its support on the floor of Congress." It was something Jefferson never forgot.

In the end, Congress deleted 630 words and added 146 to Jefferson's draft. But the most famous and enduring parts of the document—the assertions of freedom and individual liberties—remained essentially Jefferson's.

Perhaps the change that most pained Jefferson was the deletion of an entire section denouncing slavery and the slave trade in America. Jefferson wrote that King George "has waged cruel war against human nature itself, violating its most sacred rights of life and liberty in the persons of a distant people who never offended him, captivating and carrying them into slavery in another hemisphere. . . ." Coming from a man who owned more than 150 slaves at the time, this passage reveals Jefferson's deep inner conflict about slavery. It was as if he was looking for someone to blame for the institution, to be forgiven for his own involvement in it. The passage was removed because delegates from South Carolina and Georgia (slave states), and even some from New England, where businessmen had grown rich from the slave trade, would not agree to it.

Was the Declaration signed on July 4?

Congress adopted the revised Declaration on July 4, 1776. But only John Hancock, the president of Congress, and Charles Thomson, secretary, signed that day, while the other members of Congress looked on. Hancock signed his name large and bold, an act of defiance—for all present knew they were putting their lives on the line. If captured by the British, they could be hanged as traitors to the Crown. Jefferson had closed the Declaration with the chilling but appropriate words, "And for the support of this Declaration . . . we mutually pledge to each other our Lives, our Fortunes, and our sacred Honor."

Then the document was whisked off to the printer to be set in type. Copies were printed and distributed to the newly minted states. In the days that followed, crowds that gathered for public

readings of the Declaration burst into wild celebration and fanfare. Bells rang, soldiers paraded, bonfires raged. After the Declaration was read in New York City on July 9, a grand statue of King George was pulled to the ground. Americans were inspired and moved by the Declaration's eloquent and powerful words. For nearly a decade, no one but Jefferson's friends and colleagues knew it was he who had written the Declaration.

It was not until August 2 that Jefferson and the other delegates present signed a copy of the Declaration that had been hand-lettered on durable parchment. When John Hancock remarked on the importance that all the delegates "hang together," or stand by their collective action, Benjamin Franklin supposedly replied, "Yes, we must indeed all hang together, or else, most assuredly, we shall all hang separately."

Who did Thomas Jefferson mean when he wrote that "all Men are created equal"?

It has been said that the United States of America was founded upon the words in Jefferson's

Declaration—that all men are created equal, and that all are entitled to the same basic rights. For more than 225 years, Americans have been debating the meaning of those words; many have struggled to ensure they apply to *all* Americans.

Jefferson was an idealist and an optimist. He saw the world as it should be, not always as it was, and in his mind he often did not make a distinction between the two. He knew that not everyone was equal in wealth, status, birth, or ability. But he did think that, ideally, everyone should enjoy equal rights.

Did Jefferson mean to include women, Indians, or blacks in this famous assertion? It's impossible to know, but doubtful. Few Americans of the time considered these people the equal of free white men. From the section about slavery that was removed from the Declaration, can we guess that Jefferson meant to include blacks? How do we make sense of this, when Jefferson owned so many slaves?

Jefferson was one of many men we call the Founders who owned slaves. He opposed slavery in theory, saying it was bad for the master and bad for the slave. But in practice he knew he needed slaves to work his land and help run his household. He also saw himself as a sort of father figure who took care of and provided for his slaves, who (he thought) were not equipped to function in white American society as capable, free-thinking individuals. It was a complex situation, one the Founders would leave for future generations to resolve.

CHAPTER 4

Jefferson Puts Virginia First

Lovely Monticello

Did Jefferson fight in the Revolutionary War?

All during the drafting of the Declaration of Independence, Jefferson had been eager to get home to the Virginia hills he called "my country." Martha still wasn't well, and he wanted to be nearby. He also wanted to be a part of important work going on at the state level: New state *constitutions* were being written to replace the English laws. If the new laws weren't good ones, what was the point of fighting an uncertain war? Jefferson knew that as the largest state, Virginia might set a model of government for other states, and the nation, to follow. Although he never fired a shot, Jefferson would "fight" most of his Revolutionary War battles in the Virginia Assembly (the former House of Burgesses), proposing laws and addressing issues that would be important to the young nation when the war ended.

What reforms did Jefferson work to achieve while in the Virginia Assembly?

Jefferson took up many issues he felt were crucial to the success of a society in which people had more equal opportunity and were equipped to govern themselves. Among them were the following:

• *Voting rights and land ownership*

In Virginia the Tidewater aristocrats held enormous amounts of land, which they usually willed in their entirety to their eldest sons. This practice, called *primogeniture*, sometimes left other children and their mother destitute, while the eldest son enjoyed wealth, status, and privilege through no action or merit of his own. (Jefferson's own father had made sure all his children and his widow were provided for in his will.) Jefferson worked to abolish primogeniture, opening more land for small farmers. Since land ownership was a requirement for voting, this also meant more Virginians could vote, diluting the power of the Tidewater aristocrats.

• *Universal public education*

Jefferson believed that for Americans to choose their own leaders and run for office themselves, everyone must have enough education to allow him to read about and understand the issues at hand. To this end, he drafted a Bill for the More General Diffusion of Knowledge. This bill proposed to guarantee three years of public schooling for all boys and girls, and higher education for the few boys who showed the most promise and ability. (Girls were not included in the higher levels because they were thought to need only enough education to prepare them for marriage and motherhood. Slaves of both sexes were excluded altogether.) This system would allow the rise of a "natural aristocracy" of talent and virtue, in place of a European-style aristocracy of wealth and birth. Though Jefferson's bill came up for vote three times between 1779 and 1817, it didn't pass. Too radical, too expensive, too unnecessary, the Assembly said.

• *Gradual emancipation of slaves and end of the slave trade*

Jefferson formulated a plan for the gradual emancipation of slaves and the colonization of these blacks elsewhere. The plan was so revolutionary that he didn't even introduce it to the Assembly. Jefferson also opposed the importation of new slaves into the state, a practice that was prohibited in a bill passed in 1778.

• *Freedom of religion*

The Anglican Church, or Church of England, was the official religion of Virginia. Though other religions were tolerated, everyone had to pay taxes to support the Anglican Church. Religion and government (church and state) had been intertwined in Europe since ancient times. But Jefferson felt that citizens' private beliefs and opinions were no business of the government; the two should be completely separate.

No citizen should be forced to support a certain church (or any church at all) or be kept from supporting another, and no one's civil rights should be diminished based on his or her religious beliefs. Jefferson's Act for Establishing Religious Freedom was introduced in 1779. After periodic debate, it passed in 1786. Jefferson viewed this as one of his greatest accomplishments.

❝ If a nation expects to be ignorant and free . . . it expects what never was and never will be. **❞**
—**Jefferson**, in a letter to fellow Virginian Charles Yancey, in 1816

DID JEFFERSON BELIEVE IN GOD?

Like many men of his time, Jefferson rarely went to church. He did believe in God, but did not like organized religions and overbearing clergymen, whom he thought had no more right than King George to control the minds of men.

Jefferson, like a true Enlightenment thinker, based his religious ideas more on reason than faith. He did not believe in divine intervention or the supernatural, or that humans could receive direction or revelation from on high.

Jefferson did follow the philosophy and teachings of Jesus, which he later gathered from the Bible's New Testament and put in a little book he called *The Life and Morals of Jesus of Nazareth*. Because Jefferson followed the core teachings of Jesus, he considered himself a "real Christian"—a truer Christian, he believed, than clergymen who had used Jesus' philosophy to create a system of organized religion that Jesus himself, "were he to return to earth, would not recognize one feature." Yet while Jefferson revered Jesus the man, he did not accept his godhood—a fundamental belief of Christianity.

What did Thomas Jefferson grow at Monticello?

If it wasn't for the duty Jefferson felt to participate in government, he would've likely devoted himself full-time to science and farming. Jefferson thought working the land was an honest, necessary, and healthy occupation. He envisioned a nation of small farmers, for these hardy, self-reliant people were the backbone of American virtue. (In contrast, Jefferson felt, city-dwelling businessmen were breeders of vice, gambling, and crime.)

Jefferson, of course, was not a small farmer but a large planter. He was the second largest slaveholder in Albemarle County, and one of the largest landowners in the state. His main cash crops were tobacco and, later, wheat. Close to the house he planted a vegetable garden that eventually stretched 1,000 feet (longer than three football fields placed end to end!). Here he experimented with 250 varieties of more than 70 species of vegetables and herbs from around the world, including nearly 20 varieties of the English pea, believed to be Jefferson's favorite vegetable. His goal was to find the best variety of each crop and get rid of the others. (He also grew tomatoes, which many Americans considered poisonous until Jefferson ate them.)

In his fruit garden and orchards, Jefferson experimented with about 170 varieties of fruit, including pears, plums, cherries, apricots, figs, strawberries, gooseberries, raspberries, currants, and two of his favorites, peaches and apples. Nearby he planted two vineyards, and around the grounds he planted more than 160 species of what one visitor called his "pet trees." Nearest the house Jefferson would later plant flower gardens. One wildflower he included was *Jeffersonia Diphylla*, also called the Twinleaf, named for him by a botanist friend.

What was so special about Jefferson's home?

The Jeffersons had moved into the main house at Monticello in 1775, but work was ongoing. Jefferson was aiming to create the perfect retreat, a practical but elegant haven of comfort designed "with a greater eye to convenience." Monticello was full of special features. Beneath the house, mostly hidden from view by raised walkways, were the service areas: the stables, carriage stalls, icehouse, kitchen, smokehouse, dairy, wine cellar, and quarters for slaves who were house servants. Above the service areas rose the brick house with its stately columns.

Jefferson would make good use of natural light, creating skylights in many rooms and some large, double-paned windows and doors that let in light but kept out cold and noise. Between the entrance hall and parlor was an elegant set of double glass doors that were connected by a chain beneath the floor; whenever one door was opened or closed, the other followed in tandem. And because Jefferson hated to lose space as much as he hated losing time, he would design alcove beds that nestled into the walls and staircases and closets that fit next to, around, and above them.

Did Monticello have a museum in it?

No detail of Jefferson's home escaped him. He chose nearly all the contents of the house, even sketching draperies and designing furniture. Perhaps the most unusually furnished room was the front entrance hall. It would become a museum of sorts, filled with maps, artwork, and one of the nation's finest private collections of natural history and Indian artifacts. In this room Jefferson greeted visitors among huge wall maps, busts of Enlightenment thinkers, copies of famous European paintings, and an engraving of John Trumbull's painting *Declaration of Independence* (see page 35). There were also moose, deer, and elk antlers; part of a buffalo skull; the bones of an extinct animal called a mastodon; the stuffed head of an American bighorn sheep; and Indian maps drawn on animal hides.

What was Mulberry Row?

Most afternoons when Jefferson was at Monticello, he inspected the work of his slaves. He started at Mulberry Row, a dirt road running

---

WORLD-CLASS HOME

Monticello is the only house in the United States on the United Nations' World Heritage List of international treasures, along with the pyramids in Egypt and the Great Wall of China. If you can't visit the house, near the city of Charlottesville, you can take a virtual tour at www.monticello.org.

alongside the main house. The row was lined with mulberry trees and log-cabin homes and workshops of house servants, skilled slaves, and hired white workmen. The dirt-floor cabins were sparsely furnished, with bedding and a few cooking utensils.

With the cabins were a stable, joinery (for making furniture), blacksmith shop, nail factory, sawmill, and combination smokehouse-dairy. Mulberry Row was the center of industry at Monticello, and it hummed with the activity of hammers, saws, and axes, and the rumble of mule-drawn carts carrying firewood, charcoal, and water for laundry. Jefferson's slaves cooked, wove cloth, did carpentry and metalwork, built the house and outbuildings, worked in the nail factory, and tended Monticello's gardens, orchard, fields, and house. Slaves who worked in the fields probably lived in small clusters of houses in or near the fields.

WAS JEFFERSON AN INVENTOR?

He was really more of an innovator than an inventor, improving on many ideas and inventions rather than devising them from scratch. The many useful gadgets found at Monticello included:

• a swivel chair that allowed Jefferson to move toward the light as he read and had candlesticks attached to the arms to give him light while reading after dark

• a revolving book stand that could hold five books

• a seven-day calendar clock that told both the time and day of the week

• dumbwaiters, or shelves that revolved or moved up and down through the walls like miniature elevators, allowing food and wine to be served from outside or below the room with a minimum number of servants entering and interrupting conversation

In addition to these items, Jefferson is credited with three original inventions:

• the moldboard (part of a plow) of least resistance, which made plowing fields easier and more efficient because it moved through soil more smoothly than other moldboards

• the cipher wheel, used to code and decode messages

• the spherical sundial, which was shaped like a globe and told the time of day

How did Jefferson treat his slaves?

Jefferson generally treated them humanely, sometimes buying and selling slaves to keep families together. He resorted to whipping or flogging (done by overseers, not himself), or selling them far away only in cases of extreme disobedience. In 1814 Jefferson wrote, "My opinion has ever been that until more can be done for [enslaved blacks], we should endeavor, with those whom fortune has thrown on our hands, to feed and clothe them well, protect them from ill usage, require such reasonable labor only as is performed voluntarily by freemen."

But Jefferson did expect his slaves to work hard—from dawn till dusk, six days a week. Evenings, Sundays, and holidays were their own time, during which some danced, sang, or held prayer meetings. Others used the time to do extra work fishing, trapping, or laboring in their own vegetable gardens and poultry yards. They could keep the fruits of this labor or sell them to Jefferson. Slaves earned one dollar (equal to a day's wage for a skilled bricklayer of the time) for: eight chickens, four ducks, sixteen dozen eggs, two turkeys, two mink skins, six fish, or fifty cabbages. When Jefferson's neighbors brought work to his shops, he offered some of his skilled craftsmen a percentage of the profit. And he rewarded those who worked most efficiently with favors like a new suit of clothes. Of course, it was Jefferson who really profited from his slaves' labor, and the small tokens he offered them were little compensation for a lifetime spent in bondage.

VOICES FROM HISTORY

❝ [Jefferson's] negroes are nourished, clothed, and treated as well as white servants could be. . . . [H]is negroes are cabinetmakers, carpenters, masons, bricklayers, smiths, & etc. The children he employs in a nail-manufactory. . . . The young and old negresses spin for the clothing of the rest. He animates them by rewards and distinctions. ❞

—French nobleman the **duc de La Rochefoucauld-Liancourt**, who visited Monticello in 1796

❝Old Master very kind to servants. . . . Gave the boys in the nail factory a pound of meat a week, a dozen herrings, and peck of meal. Give them that [worked] the best a suit of red or blue; encouraged them mightily.❞

—**Isaac Jefferson** (1775–1849?), a slave born at Monticello and trained in metalwork, in memoirs dictated in 1847

❝Though much better than I have seen on any other plantation, [the slave cabins at Monticello] appear poor and form [a] most unpleasant contrast with the palace that rises so near them.❞

—Philadelphia native **Margaret Bayard Smith**, who visited Monticello in 1809

What was the news of the war while Jefferson was at Monticello?

The Revolutionary War went poorly for the colonists at first. General George Washington's army lost New York City and Philadelphia to the British before winning a significant victory at Saratoga, New York, in October 1777. The victory marked a major turning point in the war, as it encouraged France to enter the fight against Britain. The ragtag Continental army desperately needed the foreign money, weapons, and soldiers. Within two years the bulk of the fighting would be over.

When did Thomas Jefferson become governor of Virginia?

At the worst possible time! In 1779 the state's legislators elected Jefferson governor of Virginia. Jefferson accepted the job, though he knew the timing was terrible. For the first time since the Revolutionary War had begun, the British were headed south. Virginia was nearly defenseless. The state's regular soldiers were farther north with General Washington and the Continental army. The men left at home were called into the *militia*, but they were generally untrained farmers who were ill-prepared and ill-equipped to fight. On top of that, the state treasury was nearly empty, the British market for tobacco had been lost, and other crops had failed.

WHAT DOES IT MEAN?

A **militia** is an army of ordinary citizens, separate from the regular army of professional soldiers, which may be called upon to serve in an emergency.

Jefferson was not a military thinker. He spent his two years as governor working almost nonstop to round up new troops and supplies and to devise strategies to protect the state. With Virginia's Atlantic Coast almost impossible to defend because of its many harbors, inlets, and rivers, Jefferson moved the capital from Williamsburg to Richmond, farther inland. (For Jefferson this move had the added benefit of bringing the capital closer to Monticello.) Jefferson felt heavy burdens but had little real power as governor: The state constitution required him to get approval from an eight-man Virginia Council before doing much of anything to run the state, including summon the militia.

Who was Benedict Arnold?

In January 1781 British forces under Brigadier General Benedict Arnold, the infamous American traitor who went over to the British side in 1779, landed on the Virginia coast and sailed up the James River. Underestimating the seriousness of the invasion, Jefferson waited two days to call together the Virginia Council and summon resistance forces. The delay allowed Arnold to sweep toward Richmond, leaving a rash of looted towns and burned crops in his wake. Arnold and his men burned much of the capital, destroyed

Benedict Arnold

stores of food and arms, and forced Jefferson and other government officials to flee.

Jefferson was humiliated. He wrote a frank letter to George Washington, who sent help: fifteen hundred regulars under French major general the Marquis de Lafayette, with whom Jefferson would strike up a lifelong friendship.

Did British forces capture Monticello?

A few months after Richmond was burned, British commander Lord Cornwallis ordered one of his colonels to capture Jefferson at Monticello. Governor Jefferson got wind of this from Virginia militia captain Jack Jouett, who rode forty miles at breakneck speed through the Virginia backwoods to warn him. A few Virginia legislators who were having breakfast with the governor departed. Then Jefferson sent his family to another plantation, but he didn't leave Monticello until he saw the British troops approaching through his spyglass.

The British left Monticello untouched, but Cornwallis was not so kind to another of Jefferson's farms, Elk Hill. Cornwallis burned the farm's barns, crops, and fences; fed his army with Jefferson's sheep, hogs, and cattle; and carried off horses and some thirty slaves. Twenty-two additional slaves had already run away with hopes of joining the British, who offered freedom in exchange for military service. Jefferson may have treated his slaves humanely, but not so humanely that they didn't want to be free.

What battle marked the end of the Revolution?

In September 1781 the Americans and French laid siege to British forces at Yorktown, Virginia. After holding out for three weeks, Cornwallis surrendered his entire force of seven thousand men. Except for minor skirmishes that followed, the Revolutionary War was effectively over. The end would become official when the Treaty of Paris was signed in September 1783.

What did Thomas Jefferson vow to do when his term as governor was up?

Jefferson resigned the governorship in 1781, after his second term. Though he had done his best, he hadn't been the right man to lead the state in a time of war. The military defeats during his tenure humiliated Virginia and left a permanent scar on Jefferson's record. He was ridiculed as an indecisive coward who fled from the enemy and disgraced the state. The Virginia Assembly launched an inquiry into Jefferson's conduct as governor, but no one came forward against him. In December 1781 the Assembly dismissed the rumors and inquiry and thanked Jefferson for his service.

Even before the inquiry, however, Jefferson had decided to retire from politics and public life. He soon asserted that he had "retired to my farm, my family and books from which I think nothing will ever more separate me." He still believed in duty, but he felt that he had fulfilled his charge to serve the public. And Jefferson took criticism personally. He wrote to fellow Virginian James Monroe, a young law student he was mentoring, that the charges made against his conduct as governor had "inflicted a wound on my spirit which only will be cured by the all-healing grave." To friend and Virginia legislator James Madison, Jefferson wrote, "I think public service and private misery inseparably linked together." Adding to his despair was the recent death of his five-month-old daughter and the persistent poor health of his wife. Jefferson vowed never to accept public office again.

What was *Notes on the State of Virginia*?

Thomas Jefferson played such a significant role in founding and shaping the United States that it's easy to overlook his contributions to early American science. After retiring as governor, Jefferson wrote *Notes on the State of Virginia*, his only full-length book. It was a sort of super-guidebook in which he described Virginia's beauty, natural features, wildlife, plants, history, business, population, religion, politics, laws, and customs. He also discussed the necessity of public education, the structure of Indian languages, and the future of slavery in America. His prose was often brimming with pride in "his country." He wrote of Virginia past and present, and of Virginia as he hoped it would one day be.

Notes wasn't originally intended for publication but as an answer to twenty-three questions about Virginia posed by a French diplomat. Jefferson's response grew until it reached three hundred pages. When the book was published in France, then in England and America, its important scientific observations, elegant writing, and thoughts on philosophy and government established Jefferson's reputation as a universal scholar.

What did *Notes* say about blacks and slavery?

Jefferson didn't believe the United States could retain its cherished liberties if slavery remained a part of the nation's fabric. "Indeed," he wrote, "I tremble for my country when I reflect that God is just: that his justice cannot sleep forever." In *Notes* he proposed a system of gradual emancipation in which slave girls and boys would be educated until the ages of eighteen and twenty-one, respectively, and then freed and relocated, maybe back to Africa. Jefferson was convinced that the two races could not live equally together in the southern states because blacks had been so abused by whites, and whites had such deeply rooted prejudices against blacks. Jefferson himself considered blacks to be "more generally gifted than the whites" in music and "at least as brave, and more adventuresome." But he also felt they were "in reason much inferior . . . and that in imagination they are dull." These negative assertions are terribly offensive to modern readers, yet in the American South in Jefferson's day, slavery was a way of life that most whites took for granted as reflecting the natural order of things. That Jefferson would concede that blacks were superior to whites in anything, and that he would argue for emancipation, was exposing himself to ridicule. He did not have Notes widely distributed in Virginia.

> ### SIZING UP AMERICA
>
> In *Notes* Jefferson discounted claims that North American wildlife was smaller and inferior to that of Europe. To prove his point, he went so far as to have a moose skin, skeleton, and horns shipped to French naturalist Georges de Buffon in 1787!

What left Jefferson with a "blank which I had not the spirits to fill up"?

In May 1782 Martha gave birth to a daughter named Lucy. The baby was healthy, but Martha was dangerously ill. Each pregnancy had claimed more of her strength, and this delivery had been especially difficult. For four months Jefferson tended his wife and was never out of earshot. Yet Martha grew steadily weaker. On September 6 Jefferson lost the person he called "the cherished companion of my life."

So deep was his grief over Martha's death that he paced day and night, not leaving his room for three weeks. When he finally emerged, his primary activity was riding horseback through the woods with ten-year-old Patsy by his side. "In those melancholy rambles," Patsy later wrote, "I was his constant companion, a solitary witness to many a violent burst of grief." It was months before Jefferson began to come out of what he described as "the stupor of mind which had rendered me as dead to the world as was she whose loss occasioned it."

CHAPTER 5

An American in Paris

Jefferson as minister to France

Why did Jefferson return to politics after his wife's death?

In 1783 Congress asked Jefferson to go to France and help John Adams and Benjamin Franklin negotiate the peace treaty with Britain. Jefferson accepted. His mind needed useful occupation and distraction from his sorrow. Patsy would accompany him, while Polly and Lucy stayed in Virginia with Martha's half sister Elizabeth Eppes and her family.

Ever-curious Jefferson was eager to visit Europe, but weather and travel delays kept him and Patsy from departing. By the time they could leave, a provisional treaty had been signed in Paris and the delegation no longer needed his help. The Virginia Assembly took the opportunity to elect him to Congress, a post he also accepted.

Who was president while Jefferson was in Congress?

The Articles of Confederation, adopted by Congress in 1781, were the framework for America's first national government. Under the Articles, there was no president of the United States and no national courts. There was only Congress, and even it didn't have much power. Why? After their recent experience being controlled by Britain, Americans were wary of any government with too much power. So Congress formed a *confederation*, or a loose association of nearly independent states. Under the Articles of Confederation, the states had more power than the national government. Each state made its own rules. Without a central authority, the national government was confusing and inefficient. But Congress did manage to address some significant issues, most of which Jefferson—now an older, senior lawmaker—was involved in.

What did the United States get out of the Treaty of Paris?

The Treaty of Paris, signed on September 3, 1783, officially ended the Revolutionary War and recognized the United States of America as an independent nation. The British gave the United States the land east of the Mississippi River, north to Canada, and south to the border of present-day Florida.

Jefferson was appointed chairman of a committee to propose what should be done with the vast new territory called the Northwest, between the Ohio and Mississippi Rivers. Jefferson proposed that Congress manage the land as several territories, each of which would become a state when its population reached twenty thousand. These states would be equal to—not colonies of—the original states. This set an important example for how newly acquired territory would be dealt with in the future. Equally important, Jefferson proposed that slavery be banned in all western lands, not just the Northwest, after 1800. This part of Jefferson's plan, which could conceivably have prevented the American Civil War (1861–1865), fought largely over the extension of slavery, was defeated by a single vote. The rest of the plan was caught up in debate and never passed. However, his ideas became the foundation for the Northwest Ordinance of 1787, which laid out how the new territories would become states and prohibited slavery in the Northwest.

What did Jefferson do in Congress that made a lot of "cents"?

Under the Articles of Confederation, each state printed its own money. Congress printed money too, and coins of many European nations circulated as well. The new nation needed a new currency. Jefferson wanted it to be simple and easy to calculate. He devised the monetary system we use today, with the dollar as its basic unit. The system, based on the decimal system of tens, was the first of its kind in the world.

Why Did Jefferson Make Sure His Daughter Patsy Was Well Educated?

Congress moved temporarily to Annapolis, Maryland, in 1783, so Jefferson left Patsy with a family friend in Philadelphia and arranged several tutors for her. Tutors were common for girls of Patsy's social standing, but less so the rigorous reading of poetry and literature he devised for her. Jefferson wanted to make sure Patsy could educate her children, because, he wrote, "The chance that in marriage she will draw a blockhead, I calculate at about fourteen to one."

With his wife gone, Jefferson focused his love, tenderness, and hope for happiness on his daughters. On Patsy especially, upon whom he already greatly depended, he put extraordinary pressure to be a productive, proper, and delicate lady. When she was eleven, he wrote to her:

With respect to the distribution of your time the following is what I should approve.

from 8. to 10 o'clock practice music

from 10. to 1. dance one day and draw another

from 1. to 2. draw on the day you dance, and write a letter the next day

from 3. to 4. read French

from 4. to 5. exercise yourself in music

from 5. till bedtime read English, write etc.

I expect you will write me by every post. Inform me what books you read, what tunes you learn, and inclose me your best copy of every lesson in drawing. . . . I have placed my happiness on seeing you good and accomplished, and no distress which this world can now bring on me would equal that of your disappointing my hopes. If you love me, then strive to be good under every situation and to all living creatures, and to acquire those accomplishments which I have put in your power, and which will go far towards ensuring you the warmest love of your affectionate father.

Did Jefferson ever go to Europe?

In May 1784 Jefferson learned he was headed abroad after all. Congress appointed him a minister to Europe. He would join John Adams and Ben Franklin, who were in Paris working to negotiate treaties of commerce and friendship with European nations.

Polly and Lucy remained with their Aunt and Uncle Eppes, while Patsy accompanied her father. Jefferson enrolled her in the finest school in Paris, a boarding school, though the two spent Sundays together. Also making the journey from Virginia were William Short, Jefferson's personal secretary, and a nineteen-year-old slave named James Hemings, who was to learn the "art of cookery" from a fine Parisian chef.

The group had barely arrived in Paris when Jefferson realized their simple American clothing was unacceptable for court life. Summoning the tailor, dressmaker, hatmaker, and shoemaker, Jefferson bought clothes for Patsy, James Hemings, and himself. Hat, French lace ruffles, and a new dress sword were all part of his ambassador's ensemble.

Where did Jefferson live in Paris?

Jefferson eventually settled into beautiful quarters on the Champs-Elysées, a boulevard lined with villas and private gardens. Despite his modest salary, he remodeled two rooms in his rented house, furnished the dwelling extravagantly, and outfitted a splendid coach. He also bought silverware, candlesticks, fine wine, books, paintings, and sculpture. As his list of belongings grew, so did his debt.

Jefferson entertained lavishly, as he was expected to as a diplomat. He was reunited with the Marquis de Lafayette, which opened doors to the upper crust of French society. Jefferson's house became a favorite gathering place of distinguished artists, musicians, men of science, and young French officers who had served in the Revolution. Though Franklin was the most famous American of his day and was extremely popular among the French, Jefferson too was well regarded for his broad intellect and political writings.

How successful were the American ministers in Europe?

Franklin, Adams, and Jefferson found that few European countries were interested in making alliances with the untried nation—one born of rebellion against a European monarchy, no less. "There is a want of confidence in us," Jefferson noted. The only country with which the Americans were able to open trade was Prussia (part of present-day Germany). Adams and Jefferson were able, however, to secure from Dutch bankers a desperately needed loan, which the United States used to pay debts incurred by the war.

Adams and Franklin did not get along, so Jefferson often found himself playing mediator between the two. He grew closer to both men in Paris. The Adams family, especially, was a great source of support when Jefferson got word in January 1785 that his two-year-old daughter Lucy had died of whooping cough. Jefferson fell into silence. He determined to have six-year-old Polly join him in France, and she finally arrived in Paris in 1787. She was accompanied by a fourteen-year-old slave named Sally Hemings, the sister of James.

What event left Jefferson "in the dumps"?

FREE IN FRANCE

Slavery was illegal in France, so James and Sally Hemings were considered free there. Jefferson paid them wages and knew he could not hold them against their will. James and Sally could have stayed in France when Jefferson returned to America in 1789. But both agreed to return to America with Jefferson on certain conditions. James secured a promise that if he taught a Monticello servant all he'd learned about French cookery, he would be given his freedom. James was freed in 1796 and given money to go to Philadelphia, where he had chosen to live. Sally agreed to return to Virginia only after Jefferson promised to free her children when they turned twenty-one.

In 1785 John Adams was appointed the first United States minister to Great Britain. Jefferson would remain in Paris as minister to France, while the eighty-year-old Franklin returned to America.

When the French foreign minister asked if he was replacing Franklin, Jefferson replied, "No one can replace him, Sir; I am only his successor." Jefferson considered Franklin, whose broad range of interests and talents paralleled his own, second only to George Washington among American greats of the revolutionary generation.

Jefferson would miss having the expertise of both men at his fingertips. And though Jefferson said the

Adamses' departure left him "in the dumps," the two remaining ministers would stay in close touch across the English Channel. They exchanged advice, offered support—and shared humiliations. When Jefferson visited Adams in London in 1786, Adams presented his American colleague at the court of King George III. The king showed what he thought of the two infamous rebels by haughtily turning his back on them.

Who was Maria Cosway?

In August 1786 Jefferson was introduced to English painters Richard and Maria Cosway. Although Maria was married, the forty-three-year-old widower fell in love with her. Just twenty-seven years old, Mrs. Cosway was a talented painter and accomplished

musician who played both harp and harpsichord.
She was small and feminine, with a head full of
curls. For the next several weeks, Jefferson and
Maria toured Paris and the surrounding countryside.
Jefferson hadn't been so happy since the death of
his beloved Martha.

In mid-September the two were out walking when
Jefferson leaped a fence and landed on his right
arm, breaking his wrist. Two weeks later Maria and
her husband had to leave Paris. Over five days
Jefferson uncharacteristically poured out his soul to
Maria in a twelve-page letter written painstakingly
with his left hand. The letter, composed as a
dialogue between Jefferson's Head and his Heart—
reason and emotion—is one of history's notable love
letters. In the end the Head wins out, as Jefferson
knew it must.

Letters passed between Maria and Jefferson, and
they saw each other again when Maria was in Paris
for several months the following fall. And though
the romance eventually petered out, the two
continued to write sporadically for many years.

What treat did Jefferson discover in Europe?

In 1787 Jefferson toured southern France and
northern Italy, seeking knowledge and inspiration to
bring home to America. He was especially eager to
see examples of classical architecture, which he had
read so much about. In the French city of Nîmes he
saw a Roman temple, the Maison Carrée, which
provided the inspiration for the Virginia capitol in
Richmond. The capitol, in turn, inspired a revival of
classical architecture in America, as Jefferson hoped

it would. He thought the new nation should have buildings that evoked freedom, harmony, permanence, and vitality.

In northern Italy Jefferson studied crops he hoped could be grown in the American South: olives, oranges, almonds, and upland rice, seeds of which he put in his coat pocket and smuggled out—an act he knew was forbidden "on pain of death." Near Milan he visited dairies to see how Parmesan cheese was made. He also learned to make vanilla ice cream and returned to America with a written recipe for the frozen treat.

Did Thomas Jefferson help start a revolution in France?

In 1788, inspired by Enlightenment ideas and the American Revolution, common people in France began agitating for individual rights. The Marquis de Lafayette wrote a Declaration of the Rights of Man and of the Citizen, a document to which Jefferson contributed many ideas. The Declaration would eventually serve as the basis for the French constitution and for similar documents in other European nations.

In response to growing unrest, French King Louis XVI began gathering troops at his palace at Versailles. Angry crowds took to the streets of Paris. On July 14, 1789, a mob stormed and captured the Bastille, a hated royal prison and symbol of the king's power. Its seven prisoners were freed, its commander killed. More angry throngs took over Paris. The French Revolution had begun.

What was the Reign of Terror?

Jefferson was thrilled by the historic events swirling around him. He cautioned moderation in the move toward self-government, however, for France had lived with tyrannical monarchs for so long that he didn't believe the people were prepared to govern themselves the same way Americans were. Though Jefferson was initially shocked by, but not disapproving of, the mob violence, he believed in the cause and its ultimate triumph.

But Jefferson only supported the French Revolution as long as it supported the rights of man. In the years that followed, the revolution would become less rational and much more bloody. In 1791 the people overthrew King Louis XVI and his wife, Marie Antoinette, demanding freedom and equality. The king and queen were imprisoned, the monarchy abolished, and a *republic* established. The following year the king and queen were tried for treason and executed. Radicals then took control of the government and began a Reign of Terror, beheading thousands of French nobles and anyone else who opposed the revolution. Tyrannical rule returned, first under a man named Maximilien Robespierre, then under the military general Napoléon Bonaparte. Napoléon took over the French army in 1796; he took control of the government in 1799 and declared himself dictator in 1804.

WHAT DOES IT MEAN?

A **republic** is a nation in which the citizens elect representatives to govern and make laws on their behalf. The United States is a republic.

What was Shays's Rebellion?

In November 1786 an army of poor Massachusetts farmers led by a Revolutionary War captain named Daniel Shays rebelled against higher taxes by attacking courts around the state. Some Americans thought this uprising was outright disrespect for state authority. Jefferson, however, saw it as an expression of discontent that had to be tolerated in a free society, to keep the government accountable. Though Jefferson never liked violence, he told James Madison, "I hold it that a little rebellion now and then is a good thing, and as necessary in the political world as storms in the physical. . . . It is a medicine necessary for the sound health of government."

AMERICAN VOICES

❝ The tree of liberty must be refreshed from time to time with the blood of patriots and tyrants. ❞
—**Jefferson**, in a letter to John Adams's son-in-law William Stephens Smith, in 1787

While Jefferson was advising the marquis in France, who was he advising at home?

In America it had become clear that the Articles of Confederation did not provide a strong enough national government. Under the Articles, Congress could not impose taxes, regulate trade, or enforce or interpret national laws.

Jefferson's mentor,
James Madison

In the summer of 1787, delegates from every state but Rhode Island came to Philadelphia for a Constitutional Convention. After a great deal of debate and compromise, the delegates produced the Constitution we still use today. The U.S. Constitution lays out the powers of the *federal*, or national, government and leaves the rest to the states.

Jefferson's friend James Madison was especially influential at the convention. Madison guided the debates and wrote down what went on, earning the title Father of the Constitution. Madison wrote letters to keep Jefferson abreast of events, while Jefferson sent Madison books and ideas about how he thought the Constitution should be framed. He expressed some reservations about the absence of term limits, especially for the newly created office of president; a president who could be reelected for his lifetime wasn't healthy for the country. (Term limits were finally set in 1951.) Jefferson also felt strongly that a Bill of Rights stating the rights of American citizens must be added to prevent abuses by the government or other citizens.

How many branches of the federal government exist under the Constitution?

To provide balance and power sharing within the federal government, the framers (writers) of the Constitution divided the government into three branches:

- the *legislative*, or the two houses of Congress (Senate and House of Representatives)

- the *executive*, led by the president

- the *judicial*, or courts

The framers created a system of checks and balances in which each branch can "check" the others to ensure a "balance" among the three branches. For example, the president can *veto*, or refuse to enact, a law passed by Congress. The Supreme Court can declare a law *unconstitutional*, or illegal.

In 1791, three years after the Constitution went into effect, a Bill of Rights was ratified. The Bill consists of the first ten *amendments*, or changes, to the Constitution, and guarantees basic liberties like freedom of speech and of the press, freedom of religion, and the right to trial by jury.

Did Jefferson get homesick for America?

Despite his usual distaste for cities, he enjoyed the culture and refinement of Paris. He loved French food, wine, art, music, and manners.

But Jefferson loved America more. He disliked the way the French rich preyed upon the poor, and he detested kings and nobles. "I was much an enemy to monarchy before I came to Europe," he wrote to George Washington. "I am ten thousand times more so since I have seen what they are." Jefferson only became stronger in his view that government should be the voice of the people. Living abroad made him more American.

AMERICAN VOICES

66 How little do my countrymen know what precious blessings they are in possession of, and which no other people on earth enjoy. I confess I had no idea of it myself. 99

—**Jefferson**, writing about American freedoms in a letter to James Monroe, in 1785

What did Jefferson discover at home?

Though Jefferson was tempted to stay in France and experience the second revolution of his life, he thought it best to get Patsy and Polly (who now called herself Maria) home safely. He applied for a six-month leave of absence during which to take the girls home. Jefferson, his daughters, and James and Sally Hemings departed in the fall of 1789. Following them on other ships were eighty-six crates of furniture, books, paintings, and gifts that Jefferson had bought in Europe.

Upon landing in America after five years abroad, Jefferson learned he'd been appointed secretary of state for the first national government under the U.S. Constitution. George Washington had been elected president, John Adams vice president. Jefferson had planned to return briefly to France and then retire from politics for good.

Would he accept the new job?

CHAPTER 6

Party Man

Secretary of State
Thomas Jefferson

What did George Washington keep in his presidential cabinet?

As Washington prepared to assume the presidency, he assembled a *cabinet*, or a group of advisors to help him make decisions on important issues like foreign affairs, war, and money matters. As secretary of state, Jefferson would be part of this circle of intimate advisors. His duties would include supervising the nation's foreign affairs and running the Patent Office and U.S. Mint.

For two months Jefferson wrestled over whether to accept the job. In the end he couldn't refuse George Washington, a man whom he greatly admired and who had himself accepted the presidency despite his strong desire to retire to his farm.

Jefferson stayed at Monticello long enough to see Patsy married to Thomas Mann Randolph, son of the Thomas whom Jefferson had grown up with at Tuckahoe. In March he departed for the nation's temporary capital, New York City.

Did Jefferson throw parties as secretary of state?

During Washington's administration, political *parties*, or groups with certain ideas about how a government should be run, began to emerge. Washington warned against parties, or "factions," as they were called at the time, but they originated in his own cabinet. As his advisors confronted the issues facing the new government, they realized they didn't agree on very basic ideas about who should hold the power, or how much, and how the government should work.

On one side of the party line was Jefferson; on the other were John Adams and Alexander Hamilton, Washington's secretary of the treasury. Hamilton and Jefferson had opposing views on nearly every issue. In large part these differences stemmed from different views of human nature: Jefferson thought people were naturally good; Hamilton thought they were naturally untrustworthy. Hamilton favored a strong federal government run by a small number of professional politicians. He believed the upper classes should lead the nation because the masses of ordinary Americans (whom he called "a great beast") lacked the ability to govern wisely. Hamilton envisioned a nation of businessmen and favored forging alliances with Britain. People who agreed with him were called *Federalists*.

Jefferson thought Hamilton's views were a betrayal of the ideas fought for in the revolution. Jefferson believed in a small federal government in which most of the power was left to the states, where more people—mostly small farmers, not Hamilton's bankers and merchants—could be involved. Jefferson and other Antifederalists, also called *Republicans*, championed individual rights and believed that ordinary Americans could, and should, govern themselves. Republicans were ardently anti-British but friendly toward America's long-term ally, France.

WHAT'S IN A NAME?

Today America's two main political parties are Democratic and Republican. But Jefferson's Republican party didn't evolve into today's; instead, it changed into the Democratic-Republican party, which in 1844 became simply Democratic.

The Federalist party collapsed in 1824. The modern Republican party was founded in 1854.

Did President Washington live in Washington, D.C.?

As Hamilton organized the nation's finances, he suggested the federal government assume the states' debts from the war. Southern states disliked this proposal because most of them had already paid off much of their debts. Republicans disliked the proposal because it gave the federal government control over the states' economies.

Together Jefferson and Madison helped broker a quiet deal with the Federalists: Southern states would agree to the debt assumption if the new national capital was established in a southerly location—on the Potomac River, near Virginia. While President Washington chose a site on the Potomac, the temporary capital moved to Philadelphia for ten years.

The site Washington chose was near his home, Mount Vernon. The "Federal City," then called the District of Columbia, was carved out of Virginia and Maryland. (In 1800, the year after Washington's death, the city was renamed in his honor.) There was much to be done to transform the swampy wilderness into an elegant city. Jefferson helped plan the new streets and buildings, even submitting his own sketches, anonymously, for a plan for the President's House (officially renamed the White House in 1902). Jefferson's plan for the house wasn't chosen, but he did work closely with architect Benjamin Latrobe to design and build another important building, the Capitol.

What other money matters did Jefferson and Hamilton dispute?

To advance his vision of a nation of businessmen, Hamilton proposed the establishment of a national bank. Jefferson opposed this idea because it enlarged the size and power of the federal government. Jefferson fought the creation of the bank on the grounds that the Constitution didn't explicitly give the government this right. (This is called "strict interpretation" of the Constitution.)

Hamilton argued that it was okay to establish the bank since the Constitution didn't specifically forbid it; he said the power was implied. (This is called "loose interpretation.")

In the end Washington deferred to his secretary of the treasury and Hamilton got his bank. Today lawmakers and judges still argue over strict versus loose interpretation of the rights granted to the government by the Constitution.

What did Jefferson do for the second time, in 1793?

Jefferson issued his resignation from Washington's cabinet shortly after the president began his second term. He was resolved to retire and be done with politics. "My farm, my family and my books call me to them irresistibly," he said. Jefferson was also tired of fighting with Hamilton and battling the Federalists, who dominated Washington's administration. Even the president himself had Federalist leanings. Washington tried to smooth relations between the two giants of his cabinet, for he valued the genius of both men. But it was no use. Jefferson finally departed for Monticello in January 1794. Hamilton resigned the following year.

How did Jefferson spend his time away from politics?

In the first spring of Jefferson's retirement, he read no newspapers and scarcely wrote a letter unless it rained. He told John Adams that he had returned to farming "with an ardor which I scarcely knew in my youth, and which has got the better entirely of my love of study."

Jefferson found plenty to keep him occupied. After his extended absence from Monticello, his lands were a mess. And he was in debt, partly because he had spent beyond his means in France. Jefferson needed to make money. Setting aside his aversion to industry, he established a nailery on Mulberry Row. His young slaves were soon turning out ten thousand nails a year.

What did Jefferson tear down during these years?

Inspired by architectural ideas he'd collected in Europe, Jefferson launched into extensive renovations of Monticello. He hoped to change the look of the house from the days when his beloved Martha had lived there. So with little concern for cost, Jefferson tore down much of what existed and started over with a new version of his mountaintop home. He would enlarge Monticello to twenty-one rooms and add such rare features as indoor toilets and a rooftop dome, modeled on the Halle aux Bleds in Paris, where he had first met Maria Cosway. It was the first such dome on an American home.

Where did Jefferson go to be alone at Monticello?

When Jefferson renovated Monticello, he reserved four connected rooms in the west wing as his private area; even his family did not enter without permission. The private rooms were a greenhouse; Jefferson's dressing room; his book room; and his "cabinet," or study, which held the desk on which he wrote the Declaration of Independence and a telescope and other scientific instruments. Jefferson slept in an alcove bed between his dressing room and cabinet, allowing him to get out of bed into either room. "Whether I retire to bed early or late, I rise with the sun," he said. First thing when he woke, he measured and recorded the temperature, the wind speed and direction, and any rainfall. Then he made a fire, soaked his feet in cold water, and dressed. Breakfast was served at eight.

How did Jefferson come to be a presidential candidate in 1796?

During Jefferson's retirement years, he never ventured more than seven miles from Monticello. He went a little stir-crazy being away from politics.

When Washington announced he would retire after his second term as president, the Republicans chose Jefferson as their presidential candidate. Jefferson never agreed to run, and no one asked him for fear he would refuse. The Republicans simply put him on the ballot. His running mate would be New York senator Aaron Burr. His Federalist opponent would be his old friend and colleague John Adams, who ran with Thomas Pinckney of South Carolina.

The election of 1796 was very different from the two before it. This time there were two parties eager to duke it out. The candidates themselves didn't do the fighting, as it wasn't gentlemanly to be involved in your own political campaign. But plenty of others did it for them. The Republicans assailed Adams as a monarchist and a friend of the British. Federalists accused Jefferson of being a godless atheist, a coward, a hopeless visionary, and a man who loved France above his own country.

Jefferson pretended not to know he was a candidate for president. (Of course he did know!) Privately he hoped Adams would win. Jefferson would accept second place, he told Madison, but he really wanted third—then he could stay home at Monticello.

AMERICAN VOICES

"I have no ambition to govern men. **"**

—**Jefferson**, in a letter to John Adams, in 1796

What surprise happened in the election of 1796?

Because of the way voting was conducted at the time, all the candidates competed against one another for the two positions. The candidate with the most votes became president, and the one with the second-most votes became vice president. In the election of 1796, Adams won first place. Jefferson, with just three fewer votes than Adams, came in second. Since the framers of the Constitution hadn't foreseen the rise of political parties, they hadn't envisioned that two opponents might have to play on the same team. But Adams and Jefferson would have to do just that.

WHO GOES TO SCHOOL AT THE ELECTORAL COLLEGE?

If you remember the presidential election of 2000, you might recall hearing a lot about the electoral college. This peculiar method of electing American presidents was designed by the framers of the Constitution, who worried about giving the common man a direct say in the presidential election. The framers also wanted to ensure that winning the presidency would require broad support from many parts of the country, not just overwhelming support from a single region.

Once eligible voters—who were almost exclusively white male property owners in Jefferson's day—cast their ballots, representatives called electors do the actual voting for president. (Together these electors, selected by various means by each state, form the electoral college.) The framers hoped the electors would choose the best candidate for the job. Once political parties arose, however, electors chose the best man from their party. In some states today, the electors are bound to vote the way the majority of the state's voters do. But others can vote however they choose (though they usually vote the way of the voters, anyway).

How well did Adams and Jefferson cooperate?

Though Adams was not as radical a Federalist as Hamilton, the party wars had opened a growing rift between Adams and Jefferson. And though at first the two seemed willing to try to work together, cross-party cooperation soon proved impossible. A few days after their inauguration, on a corner just two blocks from where they had first met and worked on the Declaration of Independence twenty-one years before, the two parted ways. As Jefferson remembered the scene, "we took leave; and he never after that said one word to me on the subject, or ever consulted me as to any measures of the government."

Even though Jefferson was vice president, he essentially became the leader of the opposition.

BACK-TO-BACK HONORS

The night before Jefferson was inaugurated as vice president, he was inducted as the third president of the American Philosophical Society. The society, founded by Benjamin Franklin, was America's most important scientific organization. (The term "science" then incorporated all forms of knowledge.) Jefferson was flattered by this recognition of his remarkable mind. He spent much of his time in Philadelphia at meetings, or with members, of the society.

How did Federalists try to muzzle their critics?

The new French government, the Directory, was unfriendly toward the United States. By 1798 French privateers were seizing American ships and millions of dollars' worth of cargo. American diplomats who tried addressing the issue with the French foreign minister were hotly rebuffed. Napoléon was gaining power, and troops gathered on the coast of France fueled a rumor that invasion of the United States was imminent. Federalists were anti-French and generally for war; Republicans were against it.

President Adams did everything he could to avoid war. At the same time, he built up the navy in case peace talks failed. Meanwhile, the Federalist-dominated Congress passed a law called the Sedition Act, which made it illegal to speak out against the federal government. The law trampled the right to free speech guaranteed by the Bill of Rights. Jefferson and his fellow Republicans were aghast. Federalists claimed the law protected the nation in wartime. In reality, it was meant to silence the Republican opposition to war and to the Federalist government in general.

Why didn't Jefferson speak out publicly against the Sedition Act?

By the nature of the Sedition Act, it was illegal to speak out against it. But Jefferson could not sit back and watch the Federalists destroy American liberties. He and Madison secretly wrote papers called the Virginia and Kentucky Resolutions, which asserted the states' rights to declare the Sedition Act unconstitutional. It wasn't up to states to *nullify*, or invalidate, acts of Congress, but the Resolutions made their point. The law was so unpopular anyway that rather than do much to silence the Republicans, it turned people against the Federalists.

Did Jefferson willingly run for president in 1800?

Jefferson was so disturbed by the Federalists' handling of the government that he actively but quietly assumed leadership of the Republican party and began a campaign to unseat Adams and the Federalists. His platform included an emphasis on states' rights; a small and thrifty federal government; and trade with all nations, alliances with none. Once again, Jefferson would face Adams on the presidential ballot. And once again, the Republicans nominated Aaron Burr to be Jefferson's vice-presidential running mate.

A GENTLEMAN'S CODE

Following a practice Jefferson began in France, where postmasters often opened and read the mail, he wrote many of his politically sensitive letters in code. (He invented the cipher wheel to facilitate coding and decoding these letters; see page 59.) To Jefferson's great distress, in 1799 an uncoded letter he'd written to an Italian friend complaining of Washington's Federalist leanings and betrayal of revolutionary principles was translated from English to Italian to French and back to English—and printed in the press. In the translation process, Jefferson's words became more scathing than in the original. The unfortunate accident destroyed his friendship with Washington. Jefferson's anguish increased when Washington died later that year. In 1814 Jefferson would write of Washington, "His integrity was most pure, his justice the most inflexible I have ever known. . . . He was, indeed, in every sense of the words, a wise, a good, and a great man."

What one word best describes the election of 1800?

Nasty. While Jefferson supervised the Republican party, directly and indirectly, from Monticello, he craftily gave money and ideas to men and publications that attacked the Federalists. One of the men Jefferson secretly supported, the notorious scandalmonger James Callender, was one of many writers who would be imprisoned under the Sedition Act for his attacks on Adams and his party.

A frenzy of malicious, ridiculous personal insults were hurled in both directions. The arguments for and against each candidate were basically the same as they had been in 1796, only raised several notches. Adams was called a monarchist who would install his son as the next president, and a vote for him was said to be a vote for war. (Word arrived in 1800 that peace talks in France had been successful, but the news was too late to affect the outcome of the election.) Jefferson was branded an anarchist who would let murder and robbery reign. He was a coward who had fled from British troops during the revolution and an atheist who would block the clergy's hopes of establishing an official church of the United States.

❝ [The clergy] believe that any portion of power confided to me will be exerted in opposition to their schemes; and they believe rightly: for I have sworn upon the altar of God, eternal hostility against every form of tyranny over the mind of man. **❞**

> —**Jefferson**, in a letter to friend and fellow member of the American Philosophical Society Dr. Benjamin Rush, in 1800

Why did it take so long to determine who'd won?

When the votes were counted, it was clear that Americans favored Republicans: Jefferson and Burr had tied for the presidency. According to the Constitution, the election was to be decided by the House of Representatives. It took thirty-six separate votes in the House to resolve the election. In the end it was an unlikely advocate who tipped the scales in favor of Jefferson: Alexander Hamilton. Hamilton hated Jefferson, but he hated Burr even more.

Mr. Jefferson was headed to the President's House.

THE WATCHDOG OF THE GOVERNMENT

Even when Jefferson was ridiculed and attacked in newspapers, he never wavered in his belief that a free press was essential to a democratic society. If the people could not speak out against the government, it would be too easy for those in power to ignore the opinions of those they were supposed to represent. In 1787 Jefferson wrote to his friend Edward Carrington, "The people are the only censors of their governors . . . and were it left for me to decide whether we should have a government without newspapers or newspapers without a government, I should not hesitate a moment to prefer the latter."

AMERICAN VOICES

66 I feel a sincere wish indeed to see our government brought back to its republican principles, to see that kind of government firmly fixed, to which my whole life has been devoted. I hope we shall now see it so established, as that when I retire it may be under full security that we are to continue free and happy. 99

—**Jefferson**, in a letter to his daughter Maria, in 1801

CHAPTER 7

President Jefferson

The President's House

What did Jefferson say in his inaugural address?

On inauguration morning Jefferson dressed in a plain waistcoat and breeches and, shunning the ceremonial swords and elegant carriages used by his predecessors, walked the two blocks to the Capitol with a small parade of militia and congressmen.

About a thousand people gathered in the Senate chamber of the Capitol—the only part of the building that was completed—to hear Jefferson's inaugural address. Only those in the first four rows, however, could make out the soft-spoken president's words. He laid out his principles of good government and called for healing and harmony: "Every difference of opinion is not a difference of principle. . . . We are all republicans—we are all federalists." Jefferson was not referring to the two political parties, but to the basic American commitment to representative government and a federal union of states. Jefferson also asserted his commitment to freedom of expression: "If there be any among us who would wish to dissolve this Union or to change its republican form, let them stand undisturbed as monuments of the safety with which error or opinion may be tolerated where reason is left free to combat it."

For the first time in the history of the modern world, power had passed peacefully between political rivals. But the two former friends, Adams and Jefferson, would not correspond for another eleven years.

What was the "Revolution of 1800"?

Jefferson later called his election as president the "Revolution of 1800," a return to the republican spirit of 1776. In truth Jefferson's "revolution" wouldn't be as radical as he imagined it, though he did make many changes.

Jefferson pardoned everyone convicted under the Sedition Act and let the law expire the following year. He cut taxes and shrank the size of the government and the navy. And despite his love of finery, he thought pomp and circumstance out of place in republican government—not to mention in a city that consisted mostly of hastily built houses, unfinished buildings, and unpaved roads. He replaced the formal receptions of Washington and Adams with small, informal gatherings where he often joined his guests wearing a threadbare vest and house slippers. Diners were seated in no particular place at the table (rather than according to rank), with no one better than anyone else. Jefferson used his presidential power wisely and with a quiet confidence, winning many hearts—even Federalists'—along the way.

Who were the Barbary pirates?

Since Jefferson's days as a diplomat in France, pirates from the Barbary States of Morocco, Algeria, Tunisia, and Tripoli, on the North African coast, had been plundering European and American ships in the Mediterranean Sea. The pirates seized cargo and captured crews, then demanded ransom for the safe return of the sailors. To keep the Barbary pirates away altogether, Europe and the United States paid them bribes. Jefferson considered this dishonorable.

Now the pirates wanted more money. Instead, Jefferson sent a squadron to the North African coast. A minor naval war dragged on for several years. Though the conflict did not end the payments, it did lessen them and win the United States some international respect.

How did Jefferson's slave Sally Hemings make news?

Nowadays we are used to shocking headlines in supermarket newspapers. But it was a different story in 1802. People were amazed when scandalmonger James Callender wrote in a Richmond newspaper that Jefferson was involved in a love affair with one of his slaves, Sally Hemings. Sally, who had accompanied Maria to Paris, was said to be the mother of several children by Jefferson.

Many people dismissed the charges because Callender was such a scoundrel. Jefferson hadn't realized when he first befriended Callender quite how unscrupulous he was. (Though Jefferson figured this out soon enough, he continued to support Callender and his attacks on Jefferson's political enemies.) Callender turned on Jefferson because the president had refused his demand to be made postmaster of Richmond. Once Callender unleashed his story, the Federalist press ran with it, publishing poems and ballads about Jefferson's intimate relations with "Monticellan Sally."

Refuting newspaper attacks, Jefferson believed, only served to reinforce and exaggerate them. He remained silent. But the scandal sprang up again and again and haunted him for the rest of his life. It still haunts his legacy today.

AMERICAN VOICES

66 It is well known that [Thomas Jefferson], whom it delighteth the people to honor, keeps and for many years has kept, as his concubine, one of his slaves. Her name is SALLY. The name of her eldest son is Tom. His features are said to bear striking resemblance to those of the president himself. . . . By this wench Sally, our president has had several children. . . . 99

   —**James Callender**, writing in the *Richmond Recorder*, in 1802

What *did* happen between Jefferson and Sally Hemings?

Though no one, including Jefferson, talked about it, it wasn't unusual for Virginia planters to father children with their female slaves. Sally herself, who was three-quarters white, was the daughter of Jefferson's father-in-law, John Wayles, and a half-white, half-black slave named Betty Hemings. That meant Sally was Martha Jefferson's half sister. Members of the  Hemings family were favored slaves at Monticello. They did light housework, ran errands, or were taught a trade they could one day use to support themselves.

It appears that Sally Hemings had six or seven children, four or five of whom lived to adulthood. These children were light-skinned and were said to look like Jefferson. And though Jefferson was often away from Monticello, he was always there when Sally became pregnant, and she never became pregnant when he was not there.

No one knows for sure whether Jefferson and Sally were more than master and slave. In 1998 genetic tests comparing the DNA of Jefferson's family with DNA of descendants of Sally's youngest child did not prove Jefferson to be the father of Sally's children.

They did, however, prove the youngest child carried Jefferson genes, so Thomas Jefferson could have fathered at least that child. (So could one of twenty-four male relatives living in Virginia at the time, seven of whom frequented Monticello.) In 1813 Jefferson's nephew Peter Carr claimed to be the children's father, but this was disproved by the DNA tests. Sally's son Madison claimed that his mother told him Jefferson was his father. This may be true, but unless more information comes to light we may never know.

What happened when President Jefferson sent his advisors on a shopping trip?

Early in Jefferson's presidency, France regained the vast territory west of the Mississippi River that it had lost after the French and Indian War. In 1803 Jefferson sent his advisors Robert Livingston and James Monroe to see whether Napoléon would sell the United States the strategic port of New Orleans, for if France ever decided to deny the United States use of the port, American trade would be crippled.

Livingston and Monroe were shocked when Napoléon offered to sell the entire Louisiana Territory, land that stretched from the Mississippi River west to the Rocky Mountains. The price: $15 million, or about four cents an acre. (Napoléon needed the money for his European conquests.) The advisors knew the deal was too good to refuse. When word of the negotiations reached Jefferson on July 3, 1803, he too was astonished—and thrilled. He worried that as president, he didn't have the constitutional authority to buy the land. But he knew that if he stuck to his strict interpretation of the Constitution, the incredible opportunity would likely be lost.

Jefferson bent his principles and bought Louisiana. It was his greatest and most popular act as president. The Louisiana Purchase doubled the size of the United States, ensuring the nation's physical greatness and fueling the dreams of its westward-looking populace.

Who were Lewis and Clark?

Jefferson had always been curious about what lay to the west, beyond the Blue Ridge Mountains. Even before the Louisiana Purchase, Jefferson had been planning to send an expedition to the Pacific Ocean.
Jefferson's personal secretary, Meriwether Lewis, and his co-captain, William Clark, would lead the expedition, later called the Corps of Discovery. In addition to the men who volunteered to serve in the Corps, Clark's slave York made the journey west.

Jefferson instructed Lewis and Clark to make careful records of the land, plants, and animals they saw; to make peaceful contact and try to open trade with Indians they met; and especially to look for a Northwest Passage, or an all-water route to the Pacific. To give Lewis the knowledge he would need,

Jefferson put him on a "crash course" in botany, mapmaking, zoology, and medicine.

In twenty-eight months the Corps of Discovery traveled eight thousand miles. They faced grizzly bears, rattlesnakes, bad weather, food shortages, sickness, overturned boats, and river rapids. With the help of a Shoshone Indian girl named Sacajawea, who joined the expedition in 1805 and served as a guide and interpreter, the Corps made it to the Pacific. Though Lewis and Clark never found a Northwest Passage, they did return with an unparalleled wealth of information and plant and animal samples. Many of the Indian artifacts Jefferson displayed in his front entrance hall at Monticello were from the expedition.

"I HAVE LOST EVEN THE HALF OF ALL I HAD."

While Jefferson was president, his daughters and grandchildren had an open invitation to visit him in Washington, D.C. He was especially delighted when both daughters, along with two of Patsy's older children, came and stayed at the President's House during the winter of 1802–03. Despite Jefferson's ever-increasing debt, he insisted on paying their every expense.

Toward the end of Jefferson's first term as president, his daughter Maria gave birth to her third child. (Maria had married her cousin John Wayles Eppes in 1797.) While Patsy had always been more like her father, Maria possessed the delicate beauty and body of her mother. In April 1804, two months after the arrival of her baby girl, Maria died. She was just twenty-five. It was midsummer before Jefferson could find words for his grief. He wrote to his old friend John Page, "I have lost even the half of all I had. My evening prospects now hang on the slender thread of a single life." His beloved Patsy was all he had of his immediate family.

Why did Hamilton cease to be Jefferson's rival?

In 1804 Jefferson's vice president, Aaron Burr, whom Jefferson hated nearly as much as he hated Alexander Hamilton, challenged Hamilton to a duel—a formal fight with pistols. Burr was angry that Hamilton had supported Jefferson for president. He grew even more furious when Hamilton defeated him in the 1804 election for governor of New York. (Burr had not received the Republicans' nomination for reelection as vice president, so he ran for another office.) Burr raised his challenge; Hamilton, to defend his honor and that of the Federalist party, reluctantly accepted. On cliffs overlooking the Hudson River, Burr shot Hamilton, who died the next day. The vice president, wanted for murder, soon fled. His career and reputation were ruined.

Did President Jefferson run for a second term?

Jefferson had planned on serving only one term, but he felt he had unfinished business as president. Though the Federalist party was losing steam, he wanted to make sure the country didn't fall back into Federalist ways. And he was riding high on the successes of his first term, especially the popular Louisiana Purchase. Running against the Federalist candidate Charles C. Pinckney of South Carolina, Jefferson was reelected by a landslide: He won all but 14 of 176 electoral votes. George Clinton of New York replaced Aaron Burr as vice president.

Did Jefferson's second term as president go as well as his first?

Jefferson's second term was dominated by foreign affairs, chiefly the struggle to stay out of war with France and England. The two old rivals were at war again, and each was pulling the United States into the conflict by capturing American ships and sailors who made contact with the enemy. The British even *impressed* American sailors, or forced them to work for the Royal Navy. Many Americans, angry that Britain was treating the states like they were still its colonies, clamored for war. Jefferson did everything he could to avoid war—even after the British fired on an American ship off the coast of Virginia, killing three and wounding eighteen.

Did President Jefferson leave office on a sour note?

In 1807 Jefferson persuaded Congress to pass an Embargo Act to prohibit American trade with

European nations. Jefferson's hope was to keep American ships and seamen out of the conflict and to do enough economic harm to France and England that the two countries would be forced to negotiate with the United States.

But the Embargo Act was a disaster. Jefferson miscalculated its effects, and it did much more harm to American trade than European. Americans lost jobs and money as businesses and farms failed. Some people smuggled goods out of the country, undermining the Act and the government's ability to enforce it. Though the embargo did eventually hurt Britain, Jefferson repealed it in 1809 as one of his last acts as president. At least, he reasoned, it had saved some lives and given the nation time to prepare for war (eventually known as the War of 1812).

In the meantime, Jefferson's hand-picked successor for president, James Madison, had won election easily. After attending Madison's inaugural ball— Jefferson's first ball since Martha's death—the former president rode home to Monticello feeling he had served his nation well.

CHAPTER 8

An Old Man, but a Young Gardener

University of Virginia campus

What was Jefferson's greatest delight in his retirement?

During his long-awaited retirement, Jefferson kept as busy as ever—reading, writing, walking, horseback riding, entertaining, tinkering, and planting. Feeling he still had much to learn about nature, Jefferson said, "Though an old man, I am but a young gardener." When he found a particularly hardy plant or tasty vegetable, he gave his neighbors cuttings of the plant so they could grow it too.

Perhaps more than anything else in his retirement years, Jefferson relished his adored—and adoring—grandchildren. In 1809 Patsy and her family came to live at Monticello; by 1818 all twelve grandchildren had shared his house at one time or another. He played board games with them in the parlor, organized footraces on the lawn, and encouraged their reading and curiosity. Jefferson's granddaughter Virginia Randolph Trist remembered quiet evenings spent together reading by candlelight. She wrote that Jefferson "took up his book to read; and we [grandchildren] would not speak out of a whisper, lest we should disturb him, and generally we followed his example and took a book; and I have seen him raise his eyes from his own book, and look round on the little circle of readers and smile."

AMERICAN VOICES

66 One of our earliest amusements was in running races on the terrace, or around the lawn. He placed us according to our ages, giving the youngest and smallest the start of all the others by some yards, and so on; and then he raised his arm high, with his white handkerchief in his hand, on which our eager eyes were fixed, and slowly counted three, at which number he dropped the handkerchief, and we started off. . . . **99**

—Jefferson's granddaughter **Virginia Randolph Trist**

What kinds of guests came to Monticello?

Everyone, it seemed, wanted to meet the "sage of Monticello." One of Jefferson's family members said there were "persons from abroad, from all the States of the Union. . . . People of wealth, fashion, men in office, professional men military and civil, lawyers, doctors, Protestant clergymen, Catholic priests, members of Congress, foreign ministers, missionaries, Indian agents, tourists, travelers, artists, strangers, friends." Some of these guests, many of them uninvited, stayed for weeks. Sometimes there were fifty at a time.

Jefferson was a gracious host. Even though he was sinking deeper into debt, he refused to serve his guests anything less than fine wine and French cuisine.

What did Jefferson write during his retirement?

When Jefferson was seventy-seven, he began writing his autobiography. He wrote up through his days in Paris, then got tired of writing about himself and abandoned the project.

But he had plenty of other things to write: letters. He received so many—1,267 in 1821 alone—that he complained of the long hours he spent "drudging at the writing table." Jefferson was compelled to answer every one "with due attention and consideration," even though many of them required elaborate research. The wrist Jefferson had broken in Paris had never set right, and it gave him great pain.

The greatest correspondence of Jefferson's retirement was with John Adams, with whom he happily resumed contact in 1812. Despite their past political rivalry and different opinions about government, neither man had forgotten the other's support during the toughest revolutionary times. Now they reminisced about their contributions to the nation's history and discussed philosophy, religion, their families, aging, and current political issues. In contrast to Jefferson's friendship with Madison, which was reserved and rather formal, his relationship with Adams was spirited and dynamic: Adams would prod Jefferson and try to engage him in debate (though Jefferson characteristically dodged any question or topic he didn't want to discuss).

What cherished possession did Jefferson sell in 1815?

While Madison was president, war finally broke out between the United States and Britain. During the War of 1812, which lasted from 1812 to 1815, the British burned several government buildings in Washington, D.C., including the Library of Congress. This library, then numbering three thousand volumes, was a place for lawmakers to read, study, and borrow books. (Today, the Library of Congress is also open to researchers and other visitors and is the largest library in the world.)

Jefferson offered his own treasured 6,487-volume library to replace the burned books. His library, one of the largest and finest in the country, covered every branch of human learning and included books in English, French, Spanish, Italian, Greek, Latin, and Anglo-Saxon—all the languages that Jefferson read. Congress paid Jefferson $23,950, about half of what his library was worth, which Jefferson used to pay off debts. But he soon wrote to John Adams, "I cannot live without books." Ignoring the fact that he could not afford it, Jefferson began collecting another library.

What labor of love did Jefferson call the "last service I can render my country"?

Jefferson's plan for universal public education had not passed, but he never stopped working to educate America's future generations. Jefferson began building Central College in nearby Charlottesville in 1817, two years before the Virginia legislature agreed to establish the school as the state-supported University of Virginia. It would be the first public university open to people of all religions.

Jefferson was the university's architect in every way: He designed the school's buildings and grounds, oversaw its construction and planting, organized its curriculum, and chose most of its professors. His "academical village" was built on a quadrangle of land where students and faculty would live close together—a unique arrangement Jefferson hoped would stimulate academic inquiry and achievement. To the north was the library, housed in a rotunda—a round building with a domed roof. The southern end of the quadrangle was left open to the view of the mountains, a symbol of the freedom of the human mind.

Jefferson rode down his mountain to the site regularly to supervise the goings-on. In the evenings he could view the construction from Monticello with his telescope. Jefferson was the university's first head of school when it opened in 1825. The founding of the university was one of Jefferson's proudest achievements.

❝Enlighten the people generally and tyranny and oppressions of body and mind will vanish like evil spirits at the dawn of day.❞
—**Jefferson**, in a letter to French educator Pierre Samuel Du Pont de Nemours, in 1816

Did Thomas Jefferson live to see the fiftieth anniversary of the Declaration of Independence?

Jefferson's health declined as the fiftieth anniversary of the Declaration approached, but he was determined to see the day. An invitation arrived to the Fourth of July festivities to be held in

Washington, but eighty-three-year-old Jefferson was too weak to leave home.

On July 2 Jefferson fell into a deep sleep in his bed at Monticello. The next day he awoke briefly and asked, "Is it the Fourth?" He was told that it would be, soon. At noon the next day, while bells celebrating the nation's birthday rang in the valley below, Jefferson quietly passed away.

In Massachusetts, John Adams fell unconscious in his favorite reading chair. About five hours later, he woke briefly. Not knowing his friend had gone before him, Adams reportedly whispered, "Thomas Jefferson survives." Only two hours later, Adams, too, was gone.

AMERICAN VOICES

66 All my wishes end where I hope my days will end, at Monticello. 99

—**Jefferson**, in a letter to Maria Cosway, in 1820

What did Jefferson want inscribed on his tombstone?

After Jefferson died, his family found instructions for what he wanted inscribed on his grave in the small cemetery at Monticello, "and not a word more":

Here was buried

Thomas Jefferson

Author of the Declaration of Independence

Of the Statute of Virginia for Religious Freedom

And Father of the University of Virginia

Why didn't Jefferson mention being president of the United States? Jefferson had never desired power for the sake of pure power, or public office for the sake of prestige. It was most important to him that he further his vision for his state and the nation. The intellectual achievements he noted on his grave were those, Jefferson wrote, "as testimonials that I have lived, I wish most to be remembered."

Jefferson's tombstone at Monticello

What became of Monticello after Jefferson's death?

Although Jefferson kept records of almost every expenditure in his adult life, he sank deeper and deeper into debt. As a statesman he had lived beyond his salary; as a planter he kept hoping the next crop would be a bumper. He could not rein in his generosity and love of finery, and debts from his father-in-law kept popping up. At his death Jefferson owed more than a hundred thousand dollars—equal to several million dollars today.

Jefferson lived in an extraordinary state of denial until he began to sense the end was near. "I am overwhelmed at the prospect of the situation in which I may leave my family," he wrote four months before his death. In desperation he organized a lottery to sell some of his lands, hoping enough money could be raised to save his beloved Monticello, his slaves, and some land for his family to live on. Ever the optimist, Jefferson died believing his debts would be paid and his house and slaves would remain in the family.

But it was not to be. The receipts from the lottery were not enough, and Jefferson's family was forced to sell everything—house, furnishings, and slaves. Monticello went through several owners and fell into terrible disrepair. In 1923 citizens formed the Thomas Jefferson Memorial Foundation to purchase and restore Monticello. Three years later, during the centennial of Jefferson's death, Monticello was dedicated as a public memorial.

Did Jefferson free any of his slaves in his will?

For most of his life, the man who wrote "all Men are created equal" owned between one hundred and two hundred human beings. He saw fit to free only seven of them, two during his lifetime and five in his will. All of these were males from the Hemings family, and all had learned a trade they could use to support themselves. Three other Hemings slaves (two of them Sally's children) who were light-skinned enough to pass for white "ran away" and were not pursued. Sally herself was freed by Patsy within two years of Jefferson's death.

Jefferson was a man of his times, and it's difficult to completely relate to the issues he faced. However, emancipating slaves wasn't unheard of in Jefferson's day. Other Virginians, including George Washington, did so, if not in their lifetimes, then in their wills. It's unfortunate that Jefferson, of all men—the nation's foremost champion of liberty—denied his slaves the same independence he fought to secure from King George III. We want and expect more from him.

Jefferson rationalized his involvement in slavery by telling himself that blacks were intellectually inferior to whites, and that keeping and supporting his slaves was more humane than freeing them. "As far as I can judge from the experiments which have been made," he wrote, "to give liberty to, or rather, to abandon persons whose habits have been formed in slavery is like abandoning children." Of course, freeing his slaves would've ended his idyllic way of life at Monticello. And once he grew more aware of his dire financial situation, he knew he couldn't afford to free them. "We have the wolf [slavery] by the ear," he wrote, "and we can neither hold him nor safely let him go. Justice is in one scale, and self-preservation in the other." Rather than leading by example, Jefferson left the question for future generations to tackle.

Jefferson was sure the "abominable crime" of slavery couldn't last if the American experiment was to succeed. By 1804 slavery had already been abolished in the states north of Maryland. Jefferson was equally convinced that freed blacks would have to be removed to Africa or elsewhere. Had he lived forty years longer to see the American Civil War, he would've learned that he was right about the former, wrong about the latter.

How does Thomas Jefferson live on today?

Jefferson's likeness graces the nickel and the two-dollar bill; his face looks down from Mount Rushmore and out from the Jefferson Memorial in Washington, D.C. Cities, towns, counties, and people have been named in his honor.

But the most fitting memorial of all is the enduring Jeffersonian freedoms Americans enjoy every day.

The Jefferson Memorial reflected in the Tidal Basin

No other Founder left such an impact on the nation and its philosophy of government. His ideas about liberty extended beyond the United States as well, to influence the French Revolution and revolutions in Latin America and India.

Jefferson was a man of extraordinary talents and extraordinary contradictions. He was an aristocrat but the nation's first "man of the people." He disliked powerful governments but doubled the size of the United States with one sweep of his pen. He professed a love of farming but never plowed a field. He kept careful records of his finances but was chronically in debt. He hated slavery but owned slaves all his life.

Jefferson's character was certainly flawed. And while we wish Jefferson had considered blacks, and women, his equals, we cannot judge him by our modern standards and attitudes. Over the years, groups not originally afforded equal rights have held up Jefferson's ideals to gain freedom and equality. The history of the United States is, like Jefferson's own life, a history of striving to live up to the ideals he expressed for all time.

April 13, 1743   Born in Virginia

1757   Father, Peter, dies

1760   Enters College of William and Mary

1765   Parliament passes the Stamp Act

1766   Parliament repeals the Stamp Act

1767   Passes exams to become a lawyer; Parliament passes the Townshend Acts

1768   Elected to the House of Burgesses; work begins on Monticello

1770   Parliament repeals the Townshend Acts, except the tax on tea

1772   Marries Martha Wayles Skelton; daughter Martha ("Patsy") born

1774   Writes *Summary View of the Rights of British America*; daughter Jane born

1775   First shots of the American Revolution are fired at Lexington and Concord, Massachusetts; daughter Jane dies

1775–1776   Attends Continental Congress; drafts Declaration of Independence

1776   Elected to Virginia Assembly

1777   Unnamed son born; dies seventeen days later

1778   Daughter Mary ("Polly" or "Maria") born

1779–1781   Serves as governor of Virginia

1780   Daughter Lucy born

1781   Begins *Notes on the State of Virginia*; Americans defeat the British at Battle of Yorktown, effectively ending the Revolutionary War; daughter Lucy dies

1782	Daughter, also named Lucy, born; wife Martha dies
1783	Elected to Congress; Treaty of Paris drawn up
1784–1789	Serves as commissioner in France
1784	Second daughter Lucy dies
1786	Virginia Statute for Religious Freedom adopted
1787	Constitutional Convention held in Philadelphia
1790–1793	Serves as nation's first secretary of state
1796	Begins remodeling Monticello
1797–1801	Serves as vice president of the United States
1797–1815	Serves as president of the American Philosophical Society
1801–1809	Serves as president of the United States
1802	James Callender explodes Sally Hemings scandal
1803	United States buys Louisiana Territory from France
1803–1806	Lewis and Clark expedition travels to Pacific Ocean
1804	Daughter Maria dies
1809	Retires to Monticello
1812–1815	War of 1812 is fought between the United States and Britain
1817	Work begins on Central College (later the University of Virginia)
1825	University of Virginia opens
July 4, 1826	Dies at Monticello

Bear, James A., Jr., ed. *Jefferson at Monticello: Recollections of a Monticello Slave and of a Monticello Overseer.* Charlottesville: University Press of Virginia, 1967.

Bober, Natalie S. *Thomas Jefferson: Man on a Mountain.* New York: Aladdin Paperbacks, 1988.

Boorstin, Daniel J. *The Americans: The Colonial Experience.* New York: Vintage Books, 1958.

Brodie, Fawn M. *Thomas Jefferson: An Intimate History.* New York: W. W. Norton, 1974.

Burstein, Andrew. *The Inner Jefferson.* Charlottesville: University of Virginia Press, 1995.

Commager, Henry Steele, and Richard B. Morris, eds. *The Spirit of 'Seventy-Six: The Story of the American Revolution as Told by Participants.* New York: Harper & Row, 1967.

Ellis, Joseph. *American Sphinx: The Character of Thomas Jefferson.* New York: Vintage Books, 1996.

Fleming, Thomas. *Liberty! The American Revolution.* New York: Viking Penguin, 1997.

Halliday, E. M. *Understanding Thomas Jefferson.* New York: HarperCollins, 2001.

Koch, Adrienne, and William Peden, eds. *The Life and Selected Writings of Thomas Jefferson.* New York: Random House, 1993.

Malone, Dumas. *Thomas Jefferson: A Brief Biography.* Charlottesville, Va.: The Thomas Jefferson Memorial Foundation, 1993.

Nye, Russel Blaine. *The Cultural Life of the New Nation 1776–1830.* New York: Harper & Row, 1960.

Randolph, Sarah N. *The Domestic Life of Thomas Jefferson.* Charlottesville: University Press of Virginia, 1979.

SELECTED BIBLIOGRAPHY

Nonfiction

Brenner, Barbara. *If You Lived in Williamsburg in Colonial Days*. New York: Scholastic, 2000.

———. *If You Were There in 1776*. New York: Simon & Schuster, 1994.

Fisher, Leonard Everett. *Monticello*. New York: Holiday House, 1998.

Fradin, Dennis Brindell. *The Signers: The Fifty-Six Stories Behind the Declaration of Independence*. New York: Walker, 2002.

Freedman, Russell. *Give Me Liberty! The Story of the Declaration of Independence*. New York: Holiday House, 2000.

Lanier, Shannon, and Jane Feldman. *Jefferson's Children: The Story of One American Family*. New York: Random House, 2000.

Moore, Kay. *If You Lived at the Time of the American Revolution*. New York: Scholastic, 1997.

Fiction

Armstrong, Jennifer. *Dear Mr. President: Letters from a Philadelphia Bookworm*. Dear Mr. President Series. New York: Winslow Press, 2000.

Rinaldi, Ann. *Wolf by the Ears*. New York: Scholastic, 1993.

Turner, Ann. *When Mr. Jefferson Came to Philadelphia: What I Learned of Freedom, 1776*. New York: HarperCollins, 2003.